THE MANY WORLDS OF

BENJAMIN FRANKLIN

THE MANY WORLDS OF

BOOK TRADE AND INSTITUTIONAL DISTRIBUTION BY HARPER & ROW

FIRST EDITION

BENJAMIN FRANKLIN

BY THE EDITORS OF AMERICAN HERITAGE *The Magazine of History*

AUTHOR FRANK R. DONOVAN

CONSULTANT WHITFIELD J. BELL *Associate Librarian, American Philosophical Society*

PUBLISHED BY AMERICAN HERITAGE PUBLISHING CO., INC. *New York*

In 1787, when the Constitutional Convention began, the eighty-one-year-old Benjamin Franklin (seated, second from left) noticed a picture of the sun on the tapestry behind George Washington's chair (right) and wondered if it was rising or setting. When the convention ended successfully, he said he knew that it was rising.

6

Foreword

Americans who lived during and after the Revolution regarded Benjamin Franklin as the father of our country. Even more than Washington, he stood out among the Founding Fathers. He was the only American to sign all four of the documents testifying to our nation's birth: the Declaration of Independence, the alliance with France, the peace treaty with England, and the Constitution.

Yet by the middle of the last century, Franklin's reputation had changed; he was regarded then as the great American moralist. Mark Twain wrote that as a boy he had "had to boil soap . . . and study geometry at breakfast, and peddle my own poetry, and do everything just as Franklin did, in the solemn hope that I would be a Franklin some day."

In recent times Franklin has been looked upon as a scientist and a humanitarian. The truth is that he was all of these things. He was the Universal Man of American history, possessing an infinity of interests and an exceptional range of accomplishments. And he was born—as was our country—in an independence-minded age when a boy of wit and industry could run away from home and become a frontier hero, a businessman, or a statesman.

This book seeks in its narrative and in its authentic illustrations to capture the spirit of those times, and of that many-sided patriot.

—The Editors

Six new AMERICAN HERITAGE JUNIOR LIBRARY *books are published each year. Titles currently available are:*

THE MANY WORLDS OF BENJAMIN FRANKLIN
COMMODORE PERRY IN JAPAN
THE BATTLE OF GETTYSBURG
ANDREW JACKSON, SOLDIER AND STATESMAN
ADVENTURES IN THE WILDERNESS
LEXINGTON, CONCORD AND BUNKER HILL
CLIPPER SHIPS AND CAPTAINS
D-DAY, THE INVASION OF EUROPE
WESTWARD ON THE OREGON TRAIL
THE FRENCH AND INDIAN WARS
GREAT DAYS OF THE CIRCUS
STEAMBOATS ON THE MISSISSIPPI
COWBOYS AND CATTLE COUNTRY
TEXAS AND THE WAR WITH MEXICO
THE PILGRIMS AND PLYMOUTH COLONY
THE CALIFORNIA GOLD RUSH
PIRATES OF THE SPANISH MAIN
TRAPPERS AND MOUNTAIN MEN
MEN OF SCIENCE AND INVENTION
NAVAL BATTLES AND HEROES
THOMAS JEFFERSON AND HIS WORLD
DISCOVERERS OF THE NEW WORLD
RAILROADS IN THE DAYS OF STEAM
INDIANS OF THE PLAINS
THE STORY OF YANKEE WHALING

American Heritage also publishes HORIZON CARAVEL BOOKS, *a similar series on world history, culture, and the arts. Titles currently available are:*

CAPTAIN COOK IN THE SOUTH PACIFIC
THE SEARCH FOR EARLY MAN
JOAN OF ARC
EXPLORATION OF AFRICA
NELSON AND THE AGE OF FIGHTING SAIL
ALEXANDER THE GREAT
RUSSIA UNDER THE CZARS
HEROES OF POLAR EXPLORATION
KNIGHTS OF THE CRUSADES

COVER: *This portrait was one of the last made during Franklin's long, full life. The lightning rod and bolt recall his famous scientific experiment; the pen was his most effective weapon.*
HISTORICAL SOCIETY OF PENNSYLVANIA

ENDSHEETS: *John Trumbull's* Declaration of Independence *shows Franklin with the document's other authors: Thomas Jefferson, Robert Livingston, Roger Sherman, and John Adams.*
YALE UNIVERSITY ART GALLERY

TITLE PAGE: *On an early fireman's certificate is this ornate drawing of volunteer firemen fighting a fire in 1787. Franklin organized a similarly effective company in Philadelphia.*
MUSEUM OF THE CITY OF NEW YORK

Contents

ILLUSTRATED WITH PRINTS,
PAINTINGS, DRAWINGS, AND
ENGRAVINGS OF THE PERIOD

The maxims of Poor Richard circle this old engraving illustrating "Industry."

1

The Runaway Apprentice

On a night late in March, 1722, Boston, the largest city in colonial America, lay still and snug beneath the steeples of its fourteen churches. The flicker of lanterns that hung before every seventh building reflected dimly from the windows of the closely grouped houses. Most of the port's fourteen thousand God-fearing citizens were indoors, sheltering themselves from the cool dampness of the seaside spring.

Not so a sixteen-year-old boy, who walked rapidly and with an air of purpose through the evening. He approached the door of a shop on Queen's Street, looked around to make sure he was unobserved, and then slipped a paper under the door and hurried away.

The boy was Benjamin Franklin. The paper was an essay he had written for a newspaper published in the shop. His method of submitting his contribution for publication was thoroughly unconventional, but Ben had good reasons. He worked in the shop and his brother owned the newspaper. As an apprentice printer, Ben was not supposed to write for the newspaper. His work was washing, sorting, and setting type, pulling the long lever of the printing press, delivering the printed papers each Thursday, taking advertisements and orders for printing, and doing all the odd jobs that his older brother required of him.

His was supposed to be a mundane

When Franklin ran away from Boston and landed in Philadelphia, he was hungry and weary. But this sentimental painting shows him walking confidently down the brick sidewalk with rolls under his arm.

job, not a creative one. But he would not have it that way. From his early childhood, Benjamin Franklin rebelled against the conventional. His rebellion, born of a rare personal energy and curiosity, also reflected the political, social, and scientific stirrings of the time and place in which he lived.

This unrest was already starting to ferment in Boston when Franklin was born there, on January 17, 1706. From the earliest days of the Massachusetts colony, the Puritan ministers had controlled all phases of private life and had dominated public affairs. They still did; the great father-and-son team of clerics, Increase and Cotton Mather, ordered obedience from the pulpit in forceful sermons. But a new spirit was awakening, a spirit that called for change, and defiant voices were beginning to be heard. These voices became louder and more meaningful to Ben as he grew up.

Ben was the fifteenth of seventeen children of the poor but respected candlemaker Josiah Franklin. Persuaded by friends that the boy, his tenth son, was unusually bright, Josiah hoped Ben would become a minister and sent him to grammar school when he was eight. But Josiah later decided that he could never afford to give his son the college education the ministry required, and so, after a year, he transferred Ben to a school specializing in writing and arithmetic. "I acquired fair writing pretty soon," wrote Franklin in his autobiography,

"but I failed in the arithmetic, and made no progress in it. At ten years old I was taken home to assist my father in the business." This was the end of Franklin's formal education.

Ben soon let his father know that he had little liking for cutting wicks and pouring wax; candlemaking was not for him. Somewhat indulgently, Josiah took his discontented offspring on walks through the streets of Boston to watch craftsmen at their work with the hope of finding a trade that would interest the boy. There was a building boom in Boston; many drab wooden dwellings of earlier days were being replaced by narrow brick structures, and construction jobs were plentiful. But Ben had no interest in becoming a carpenter, bricklayer, or metal worker. The excursions, however, did have some effect. Years later he wrote, "It has ever since been a pleasure to me to see good workmen handle their tools; and it has been useful to me, having learnt so much by it as to be able to do the little jobs myself in my house when a workman could not readily be got, and to construct little machines for my experiments. . . ."

What Ben really wanted was to go to sea. Ships fascinated him, and he became a competent small-boat handler. ". . . When in a boat or canoe with other boys," he wrote, "I was commonly allowed to govern [steer], especially in any case of difficulty." He was also an excellent swimmer. As a boy, he invented a set of swimming

The last son of Josiah Franklin was born—on a bitter cold day, tradition has it—in the house below, on Milk Street in Boston. In 1820, ten years after the building burned down, this drawing was made from an earlier pencil sketch. The painting at right is thought to be a portrait of Benjamin's mother, Abiah Franklin, Josiah's second wife.

14

Boston, the wind-swept, seafaring community of Franklin's birth and boyhood, is depicted in this eighteenth-century primitive painting. The town's simple buildings stand in clusters beside its busy harbor.

AN
Historical ACCOUNT
OF THE
SMALL·POX
INOCULATED
IN
NEW ENGLAND,
Upon all Sorts of Persons, *Whites, Blacks,*
and of all Ages and Constitutions.

With some Account of the Nature of the
Infection in the NATURAL and INOCULATED
Way, and their different Effects on HUMAN
BODIES.

With some short DIRECTIONS to the UN-
EXPERIENCED in this Method of Practice.

Humbly dedicated to her Royal Highness the Princess of WALES,
By *Zabdiel Boylston,* F. R. S.

The Second Edition, Corrected.

LONDON:
Printed for S. CHANDLER, at the Cross-Keys in the Poultry.
M. DCC. XXVI.

Re-Printed at BOSTON in N. E. for S. GERRISH in
Cornhil, and T. HANCOCK at the Bible and Three Crowns
in Annstreet. M. DCC. XXX.

Cotton Mather (right), the pious and often arrogant Puritan minister, was a power to be reckoned with in Boston. He was preaching the use of inoculations to fight a smallpox epidemic, in the face of opposition by nearly all of Boston's doctors, when Ben's brother James reck-lessly leaped into the fray—on the side of the doctors. James ran vio-lent anti-inoculation letters, such as the one below, in his newspaper, The New England Courant. One doctor who did support Mather was Zabdiel Boylston, author of the quaintly titled pamphlet at left.

[Nº 4

THE
New-England Courant.

From MONDAY August 21. to MONDAY August 28. 1721.

— *Dehinc ut quiescant Moneo.* Ter.

To the Author of the New-England Courant.

SIR, *the Rev. Mr. Harris*

THE Story of *Inoculation* I see finds Employment for several Hands, some labouring to maintain, while others strive to destroy a base *Hypothesis.* And being of a publick Nature, as most Disputes are, has given Birth to several Printed Speculations, which seem on one side not so much to defend the Practice, which was ex-pected, and that justly, as on the other to condemn it as Male Administration, because disagreeing with the Modes of Physick, besides a little low Treatment on both sides. Verberations a...

Time they would look...

least a satisfactory & sufficient one, because several Inter-rogatories are to be made ; as, Whether you are sure of having this greater *Illness,* and whether mortal or not, and whether the lesser *Sickness,* as it is term'd, might terminate so, of which in their Places.

I look upon it very strange, believe me Sir, that there should be so many, who, blest with a sound and vigorous Constitution, should be desirous to bring up-on themselves a *Distemper,* of which themselves are afraid, and from which so many flee, that they should be so discontented when God brings it upon them, yet can be very well satisfied to bring it upon them-selves, after the new Fashion...

aids—a pair of paddles for his hands and "a kind of sandals" (forerunner of swimfins) for his feet. One windy day he used a kite to pull himself across a mile-wide pond as he lay on his back in the water. He paused occasionally to tread water and to pull on the string to keep the kite in the air.

So great was Ben's love of the water and ships that his father feared he would run off to sea. To keep the twelve-year-old boy at home, Josiah decided to apprentice him to Ben's twenty-one-year-old brother, James, who had just started a print shop. A formal contract of apprenticeship was drawn up. The document bound Ben to serve his brother faithfully, keep his secrets, and "his lawful commands everywhere gladly do." The

To the *Author of the* New-England Courant.

SIR, *B. T.* [No 3

T is undoubtedly the Duty of all Perfons to ferve the Country they live in, according to their Abilities; yet I fincerely acknowledge, that I have hitherto been very deficient in this Particular; whether it was for want of Will or Opportunity, I will not at prefent ftand to determine: Let it fuffice, that I now take up a Refolution, to do for the future all that *lies in my Way* for the Service of my Countrymen.

I HAVE from my Youth been indefatigably ftudious to gain and treafure up in my Mind all ufeful and defireable Knowledge, efpecially fuch as tends to improve the Mind, and enlarge the Underftanding: And as I have found it very beneficial to me, I am not without Hopes, that communicating my fmall Stock in this Manner, by Peace-meal to the Publick, may be at leaft in fome Meafure ufeful.

I AM very fenfible that it is impoffible for me, or indeed any *one* Writer to pleafe *all* Readers at once. Various Perfons have different Sentiments; and that which is pleafant and delightful to one, gives another a Difguft. He that would (in this Way of Writing) pleafe all, is under a Neceffity to make his Themes almoft as numerous as his Letters. He muft one while be merry and diverting, then more folid and ferious; one while fharp and fatyrical, then (to mollify that) be fober and religious; at one Time let the Subject be Politicks, then let the next Theme be Love: Thus will every one, one Time or other find fome thing agreeable to his own Fancy, and in his Turn be delighted.

ACCORDING to this Method I intend to proceed, beftowing now and then a few gentle Reproofs on thofe who deferve them, not forgetting at the fame time to applaud thofe whofe Actions merit Commendation. And here I muft not forget to invite the ingenious Part of your Readers, particularly thofe of my own Sex to enter into a Correfpondence with me, affuring them, that their Condefcenfion in this Particular fhall be received as a Favour, and accordingly acknowledged.

I THINK I have now finifh'd the Foundation, and I intend in my next to begin to raife the Building. Having nothing more to write at prefent, I muft make the ufual excufe in fuch Cafes, of *being in hafte*, affuring you that I fpeak from my Heart when I call my felf, The moft humble and obedient of all the Servants your Merits have acquir'd,

SILENCE DOGOOD.

‖*‖ *Thofe who incline to favour Mrs. Dogood with their Correfpondence, are defir'd to fend their Letters (directed to her) to the Publifher of this Paper.*

contract continued: "Taverns, inns or alehouses he [Ben] shall not haunt. At cards, dice, tables or any other unlawful game he shall not play. Matrimony he shall not contract; nor from the service of his said master day nor night absent himself." In return, James was to teach his brother the printing trade and provide him "meat, drink, washing, lodging and all other necessaries." There would be no pay until the last year.

Ben quickly adapted himself to the print shop—perhaps because printing was related to books, and books were the boy's great passion. He claimed that he had learned to read when he was so young that he did not remember when he could not read. He borrowed books where he could and spent the little money that came his way for pamphlets. He read at night, before work in the morning, and even on Sundays when, he said, "I contrived to be in the printing house alone, evading as much as I could common attendance at public worship." Ben's attitude toward religious ritual is illustrated by an anecdote of his childhood. When his mother salted the winter supply of meat, he suggested that they say grace over the entire cask so that it would not have to be said at every meal. Still, Frank-

Fourteen satirical letters, one of which is shown here, appeared in the Courant *in 1772. Mrs. Dogood, their alleged author, was obviously fictitious; but no one suspected a teenaged apprentice of being the real writer.*

lin had a deep faith in God, although he rarely went to church.

Ben used the few hours he was able to steal from other activities for writing as well as reading. He schooled himself in composition by rewriting articles from an English magazine, the *Spectator*, and was only thirteen when he wrote the first work of his own for publication. A lighthouse keeper and his family had been drowned in a storm, and Ben wrote a poem about the tragedy. His brother James printed it and sent him out in the street to sell it. According to Franklin, the poem sold rather well, although it was, he later said, "wretched stuff in the Grub-Street ballad style." Ben was encouraged in his poetry writing by his father's brother, a persistent part-time poet who regarded this nephew with special affection. Ben's father, however, thought prose a worthier—and far more profitable—literary undertaking, and it was to this medium that Ben turned for his first important writing.

In 1721 James Franklin started to publish a newspaper, the *New England Courant*. There were two newspapers in Boston already, dull sheets that blandly reported acts of the government, sermons, ship sailings, and the like. James's paper was different. He was encouraged by a group of young friends who, if they were not radicals, certainly had advanced ideas. These men submitted challenging articles, signing them with fictitious, whimsical names such as Ichabod Henroost, Tabitha Talkative, and Fanny Mournful.

Ben too had ideas he wanted to see in print, but he knew that James would not publish the opinions of his younger brother. So, in a disguised handwriting, he composed a letter to the *Courant*, signing it Silence Dogood. This was the paper he slipped under the door of the shop that March night in 1722.

In the letter he told the life story of his fictitious Silence Dogood, having prefaced the fanciful biography with the explanation that since "the Generality of People, now a days, are unwilling either to commend or dispraise what they read, until they are in some measure informed who or what the Author of it is . . . it may not be amiss to begin with a short Account of my past Life and present Condition, that the Reader may not be at a Loss to judge whether or no my Lucubrations [elaborate compositions] are worth his reading."

Silence, Franklin wrote, had been apprenticed as a housekeeper to a minister who later married her. To Benjamin this was part of his family history; his maternal grandmother had been an indentured servant who had married his grandfather. At the time Franklin created her, Silence was supposed to be a widow who had opinions and ideas on many subjects which, the letter said, she would contribute to the paper from time to time.

The day after he slipped the letter under the door, Ben listened to James

A view of New York a few years before Franklin passed
through the port shows a Brooklyn ferry pier in the
foreground. A flat-bottomed cargo ferry rests at the
landing, while seagoing ships anchored in mid-harbor
fire smoky holiday salutes, and the solid Dutch-style
houses of Manhattan stand sedately in the background.

and his friends as they praised it highly and speculated on who, among several men of wit and learning, could have written it. Such praise was heady medicine to a sixteen-year-old. He wrote thirteen more Silence Dogood letters, in which he commented on such subjects as old maids, education for women (he was for it), drunkenness, and the night life of Boston (he was against it). One letter included a vicious satire on Harvard College, then nearly a century old and the center of learning in New England.

Meanwhile, James's paper had gotten off to a fast start—on the wrong foot, as far as the public authorities were concerned. Clergyman Cotton Mather had heard about inoculation against smallpox and had convinced Dr. Zabdiel Boylston, an influential physician of the day, to try the method in Boston, where an epidemic of the disease had broken out. Two of James's friends, a young doctor and a druggist, wrote violent articles for the Courant condemning the little-known preventative as quackery and telling Mather to go back to his witch-hunting. A feud started in which Cotton Mather bitterly attacked the Courant. It was, he wrote in a rival newspaper, "a Notorious, scandalous Paper . . . full freighted with Nonsense, Unmannerliness, Railery, Prophaneness, Immorality, Arrogancy, Calumnies, Lyes, Contradictions, and what not."

One could not safely cross the powerful Mathers in Boston in the 1720's. The authorities watched the Courant closely, and when James published a humorous squib criticizing the government, he was found in contempt of the provincial council and sent to jail. While James was in prison, Ben put out the Courant, and printed in a Silence Dogood letter this excerpt from the London Journal: "Without freedom of thought there can be no such thing as wisdom; and no such thing as public liberty without freedom of speech . . . Whoever would overthrow the liberty of a nation must begin by subduing the freeness of speech: a thing terrible to public traitors." Such thinking would eventually become the cornerstone of Franklin's mature philosophy—although his eloquence at this time did little to help his imprisoned brother.

James was finally released from jail when he promised to behave—a promise which was not kept long. Soon an article in the Courant condemning religious hypocrisy aroused the wrath of clergy and council, and James was forbidden to continue publishing the paper—"unless it be first supervised by the Secretary of this Province." But the ban did not apply to Ben. James could evade the order and continue to publish under his brother's name. To effect the ruse, James publicly released Ben from his remaining four years of service—having drawn up new, secret apprenticeship contracts.

The paper prospered, but Benjamin found his apprenticeship tedious

and a curb on his growing ambition. After eight months as "publisher" of the *Courant*, knowing that James would not dare to produce the secret indentures, Franklin decided to run away. He sold his books to raise money and persuaded a friend secretly to book passage for him to New York. All of this deceit lay heavily on Franklin's conscience: it was "one of the first errata of my life," he wrote in his autobiography.

Ben sailed out of Boston Harbor in September, 1723, and in three days was in New York. This strange city of high-gabled houses built by the Dutch did not offer much opportunity for a printer's assistant. Only half the size of Boston, it had one printer in the entire town. He was William Bradford, who would later be ranked as a pioneer of American journalism. Bradford told Ben that he did not need a new hand, but that perhaps his son Andrew, who was in the printing business in Philadelphia, might be able to use him. So, without pause, Ben set out for Pennsylvania. Since he did not have enough money for coach fare or a coastal voyage, he walked across New Jersey and hitchhiked down the Delaware in a large rowboat, spending most of one night pulling on an oar. He arrived in Philadelphia on a Sunday morning, dirty and tired, with only a few copper coins in his pocket.

Philadelphia was almost as big as Boston, but more sprawling. On the

day Ben arrived, the streets were filled with "clean-dressed" people on their way to church—sober Quakers who seemed to him much like the strict Puritans of Boston. But Franklin had little inclination for churchgoing that morning. He was hungry, and he hurried to a bakery where he spent three pennies for three large rolls. Then he walked down Market Street with one of the rolls under each arm as he munched on the third. A girl named Deborah Read, who would eventually become the wife of this disheveled young man, was at the door of her home as Ben passed by and, he recalled years later, she laughed at him. Franklin ended the morning by following some of the clean-dressed peo-

Philadelphia was a bustling port when a weary Franklin docked there early one Sunday morning in October, 1723. At that time the city closely resembled this lively painting, done in 1720 by Peter Cooper, a signboard artist. It shows the homes, shops, and meetinghouses of the prosperous community on the west bank of the Delaware River. Some buildings are identified by the code at the center of the painting.

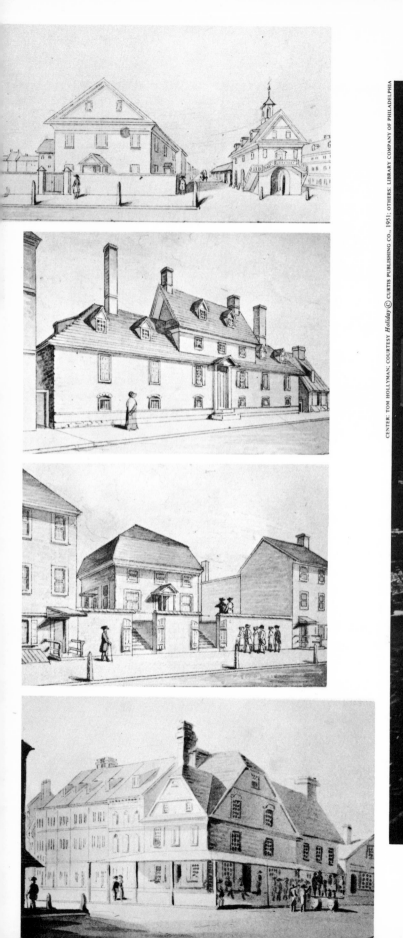

The Philadelphia of Benjamin Franklin survives in Elfreth's Alley (center), a street of eighteenth-century houses. Others that stood in the predominantly Quaker city during Franklin's time were (at far left, from top): the great Meetinghouse, built in 1695; Friends' Almhouse, 1729; Friends' bank Meetinghouse, 1685; Old London Coffee House, 1702. Above is the State House Tavern, 1693; below: a home built in 1727. All were sketched by Edward Mumford, a Philadelphia artist and engraver of the nineteenth century.

*"Having little to give, he gave expectations,"
wrote Franklin of Sir William Keith, governor of Pennsylvania (above). The amiable
but irresponsible man, who sent Ben to London, is romantically portrayed in armor.*

ple to a Quaker meetinghouse and dozing there peacefully through the meeting, his first sleep in Philadelphia.

The next morning he called on Andrew Bradford and learned that William Bradford had arrived from New York before him. Young Bradford had no work for Ben, but he told him of a new printer named Samuel Keimer who was starting a shop and might need help. The older Bradford offered to take the boy to Keimer and introduce him. If Franklin at first thought this was a disinterested kindness, he soon learned that William Bradford, who was not known to Keimer, was using the occasion to draw out his son's rival on his business prospects. "I, who stood by and heard all, saw immediately that one of them was a crafty old sophister and the other a mere novice."

Ben went to work for Keimer as a journeyman. He sorted out and conditioned as best he could the one worn set of type. He put the dilapidated press, which Keimer had not yet used, in working order. Happily independent in his new life, he was beginning to forget about Boston when he received a letter from his brother-in-law Robert Holmes. Holmes, the captain of a trading sloop anchored in New Castle harbor, in Delaware, had heard that Ben was in Philadelphia and urged the young man to go back to his worried parents.

Ben answered his brother-in-law, explaining why he refused to return home, and by chance, the letter was received by Holmes while he was with the governor of Pennsylvania, Sir William Keith. Holmes showed the letter to Keith, who was impressed by it and evidently felt inspired to aid the boy. Ben knew nothing of this, so when the governor of Pennsylvania walked into Keimer's shop one day soon afterward and invited Ben to lunch, he was "not a little surprised, and Keimer stared like a pig poisoned."

Sir William had a proposal. If Franklin went into business for himself, the governor would use his influence to get him government printing. When Ben said he had no money to set up shop, Keith suggested that he go to Boston and borrow some from his father.

Landing in Boston, Ben strode into his brother's shop, "better dressed than ever while in his service, having a genteel new suit from head to foot, a watch, and my pockets lined with near five pounds sterling. . . ." James was "glum and silent" as his brother impressed the workmen by producing "a handful of silver" and giving them "a piece of eight to drink." But Ben's visit to his father was in vain. Josiah thought Sir William wanting in common sense for proposing that an eighteen-year-old go into business. He refused his son financial support.

Ben returned to Philadelphia. When he related to the governor what had happened, Sir William waved the matter of money away. With a grand offer to finance the venture with a letter of credit, he told Ben to prepare for a trip to London to buy printing equipment. Day after day, Franklin visited the governor's mansion, hoping to be given the letter, but Keith was always "too busy." Finally, as the sailing date neared, the governor's secretary told Franklin that the letter would be sent to the ship. It was not until after the ship sailed, with Franklin aboard, that he learned that there was no letter. Keith was a dreamer who liked to make great plans and promises. When he could not fulfill them, he was ashamed to admit it.

At the age of eighteen, Ben arrived in a new city once more, once more alone and penniless. But he was not worried. He was now a journeyman printer, and London was a print-

Franklin's departure for London in November, 1724, is pictured in an imaginary scene. This woodcut shows Franklin saying farewell to a friend, while a boy carries his baggage, and a boat waits to ferry him to the ship.

HOLLEY, *Life of Benjamin Franklin*, 1848

Franklin found London both drab and exciting. Arriving there with little money, Ben first lived in the city's grimy Little Britain section which is seen at right. But he also discovered the vibrant London of the aristocratic politician Robert Walpole (above, left) and of the satirical poet Alexander Pope (above, right).

ing center. He immediately found work in Samuel Palmer's printing house in Bartholomew Close, and settled down to London life at one of its most exciting periods of literature, luxury, fashion, and wit. This was the London of Lord Chesterfield, Defoe, Pope, and Robert Walpole—a London that greatly inspired the young American printer. He read its works, borrowing books to do so, and caught glittering glimpses of it in theatres and taverns.

Franklin found London congenial. He was popular with his fellow workers, who called him the "water American" because he did not drink beer for breakfast. He impressed them and others with feats of swimming in the Thames, and taught some of them to swim. A nobleman was so enthusiastic about Ben's aquatic skills that he tried to hire him to coach his sons. Franklin actually considered staying in London and opening a swimming school, although he did not. He recognized that his stay in London was valuable; he was perfecting his printing skills and thriving intellectually. But when an opportunity came to return to Philadelphia, Franklin seized it gladly.

29

2

"The Way to Wealth"

Although Franklin tried, he never did save enough money to pay for his passage home. A Quaker merchant from Philadelphia, who had been a passenger with Franklin on his trip to London, had taken a fatherly interest in the young man, and agreed to pay his fare back to America on the condition that Franklin clerk in his store. Soon after they returned home, however, the merchant died, and Franklin was free to go back to printing.

Samuel Keimer offered Ben a job at greatly increased wages; Ben eagerly accepted, although he observed that Keimer was "an odd fish, ignorant of common life . . . slovenly to extreme dirtiness, enthusiastic in some points of religion, and a little knavish withal." Franklin soon learned why Keimer had been so generous with his job offer. The slovenly printer now had

five apprentices and indentured men; but none of them knew the business. In addition to being the master printer, Franklin was expected to whip Keimer's ill-assorted staff into shape. He did all this and more—including·the casting of the first type made in the colonies, for which he used old type to make molds. When the men became skilled under Franklin's tutelage, Keimer wanted to discharge his highly paid top hand. He provoked a quarrel by rebuking Franklin publicly, and Ben walked out. With him went one of Keimer's men, a hard-drinking young Welsh-

The hand press photographed here against an enlarged page of The New England Courant *was used in James Franklin's shop. Mastery of printing, and a deft pen, would bring Ben wide fame and early fortune.*

man named Hugh Meredith, whose father, thinking that Franklin's influence might improve his son's habits, offered to finance a printing shop for the two.

The first major expense for the new venture was an English hand press. Briefly, while Franklin and Meredith waited for it to be shipped from London, they went back to work for Keimer, who had received an order to print money for New Jersey and needed Ben's skill to handle this exacting operation. Franklin made many influential friends among the highly placed men who were on hand to oversee the printing of the money. The job was completed just before his equipment arrived from London.

In 1728, Franklin was in business for himself—soon by himself. The partnership did not last long. Meredith continued to drink heavily, and Franklin borrowed money from two friends to buy him out.

Thus, in 1730, at the age of twenty-four, Franklin started on the second phase of his life—eighteen years of unrelenting work as a businessman and artisan. As a printer, Franklin was always better than his competitors —although he never tried to do really fine work. But as a businessman, thrifty and shrewd, he was so far superior to competition that he soon dominated the printing trade in Philadelphia.

He worked day and night, usually seven days a week. He lived frugally, saving money to expand and to pay

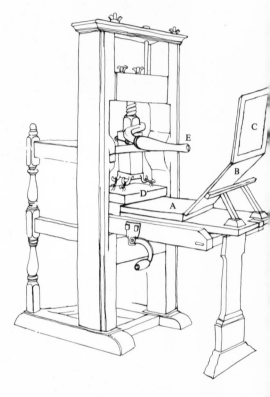

The operator of an 18th-century hand press began by inking columns of type, which were locked firmly into position on the stone (A). Next, he selected a single sheet of wet paper, secured it on the tympan (B), and covered its margins with a simple wooden frame called a frisket (C). The tympan and the frisket were folded forward over the type, and then the entire assembly was rolled under the platen (D). Finally, by pulling on the spindle lever (E), the printer lowered the platen onto the assembly (as depicted in the drawing at right), thus "pressing" the paper on the type.

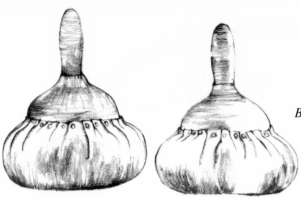

Breyers used for inking type

DRAWINGS BY JOAN BERG

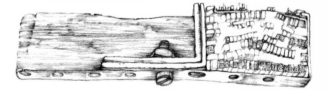

Composing stick for setting type to specified width

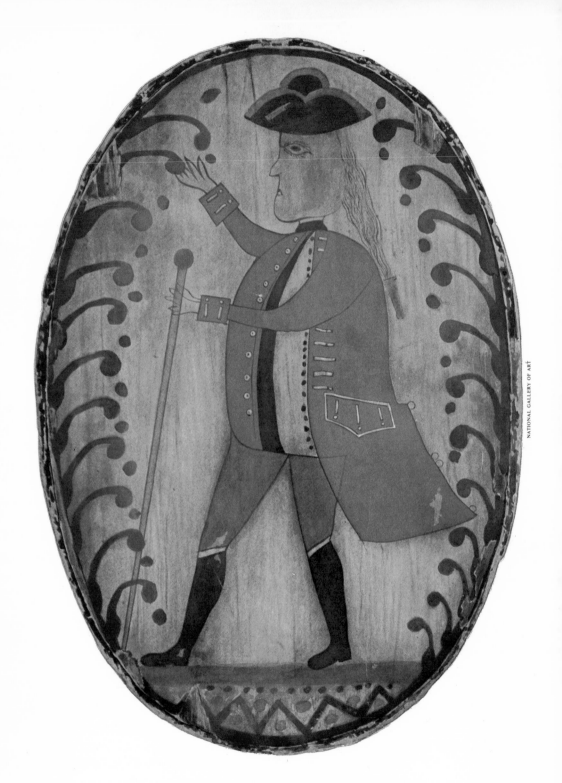

This folk-art painting of a hearty, pigtailed Pennsylvania German farmer, from the cover of an old clothes box, gives an impression of the citizens with whom Franklin dealt.

34

off his debts on the shop. Franklin dreaded debt. He considered it a form of slavery—the man who owed money was a slave to his creditor. Franklin both worked hard and saved hard, and acted the part of the industrious young tradesman to the hilt. "In order to secure my credit and character," he wrote, "I took care not only to be in reality industrious and frugal but to avoid all appearances to the contrary. I dressed plainly; I was seen at no places of idle diversion. I never went out a fishing or shooting; a book, indeed, sometimes debauched me from my work, but that was seldom, snug, and gave no scandal."

When he bought paper, he trundled it through the streets in a wheelbarrow himself to impress prospective customers. Soon influential men were talking about him in the Merchants' Every Night Club. "The industry of that Franklin," one of the members is reported to have said, "is superior to anything I ever saw of the kind; I see him still at work when I go home from the club, and he is at work again before his neighbors are out of bed."

Franklin did everything possible to get business. Keimer had an order to print a history of the Quakers which he was slow to deliver. Franklin asked them to let him print forty pages. He set and printed a page a day, redistributing the type at night—and his speed and skill soon got him more business from the Quakers.

He then turned his attention to breaking the monopoly Andrew Bradford had on government printing. Franklin reprinted an address which had been printed by Bradford and sent it to members of the Assembly. His work was so much better than Bradford's that Franklin was soon named the official printer for Pennsylvania. At this time, there was a scarcity of money in the colony. Paper money would benefit the little people, but the rich merchants were opposed to it. They wanted only hard money—coins worth their value in the metal they were made of. Franklin wrote a pamphlet entitled *A Modest Enquiry Into the Nature and Necessity of a Paper Currency*. It was so convincing that the Assembly voted an issue of paper money—and Franklin got the order to print it.

Even in this hard-working time, Franklin, as always, made friends easily, particularly among people with alert and inquisitive minds like his own. At about the time he started in business he organized ten young men—his "ingenious acquaintances" —into a club named the Junto, from the Spanish word *junta* meaning discussion group. More often it was called the Leather Apron Club because most of its members wore the work apron of an artisan. The club was a combination social group, self-improvement society, and unofficial junior chamber of commerce. Principally, members exchanged ideas at Friday evening meetings—and did a little beer drinking as well.

The Junto talked about everything.

36

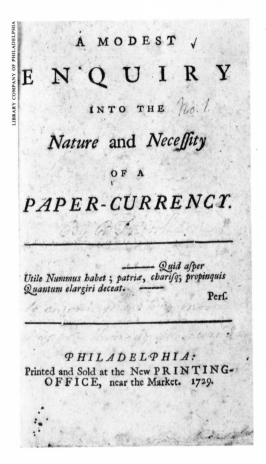

Franklin wrote the pamphlet above in 1729 to convince the Pennsylvania Assembly that paper money was sound. The pamphlet was so persuasive that paper currency was issued and Franklin was given the job of printing it. To discourage counterfeiting, he designed an intricate pattern of leaves for the bills, as on the hundred shilling note at the left.

One of the questions that Franklin threw into the discussion was: "What is wisdom?" His own answer was: "The knowledge of what will be best for us on all occasions, and of the best ways of obtaining it." Other questions, which he did not answer, included: "Is it justifiable to put private men to death for the sake of publick safety or tranquility, who have committed no crime? . . . Which is best to make a friend of, a wise and good man that is poor or a rich man that is neither wise nor good? . . . Whence comes the dew that stands on the outside of a tankard that has cold water in it in the summertime?"

The Junto's young members helped each other and the community in many ways. At Franklin's suggestion they organized the first circulating library in America, offering citizens the right to borrow books for ten shillings a year. With the money, they bought more volumes from England. "Reading became quite fashionable," said Franklin, "and our people . . . in a few years were observed by strangers to be better informed and more intelligent than people of the same rank generally are in other countries."

As his business grew and his interests expanded, Franklin decided that he should marry. He looked around for a wife, preferably one with a dowry which would enable him to pay off the balance of his debt on the shop. But he could find no such woman, for, he said, "The business of a printer being generally thought a

Deborah Read, Franklin's robust and sometimes quarrelsome wife, tended their home and helped look after the general store that Ben ran along with his print shop. The portrait of her above was done in 1759, when she was fifty-five. Francis Folger Franklin (below) was born to Ben and Deborah in October, 1732, but died at the age of four. "I have seldom . . . seen him equalled," Franklin wrote of the boy years later, "and . . . to this day I cannot think of him without a sigh."

poor one, I could not expect money with a wife, unless with such a one as I should not otherwise think agreeable." Franklin turned, in 1730, to Deborah Read—the girl who had laughed at him his first day in Philadelphia. When he started working for Keimer, before going to England, he had boarded with the Reads. He and Deborah wanted to marry before his voyage, but her mother thought them too young. From England he had written only once, to say that he might be there a long time. After this unencouraging news and before he returned, Deborah married a man named Rogers, who soon deserted her to go to the West Indies. There, it was rumored, he had died.

The young widow—if she was a widow—had no dowry. She was handsome rather than pretty; sturdy and a hard worker. She was untaught, almost illiterate, and never took any interest in any phase of Franklin's life except the home and the print shop. Their marriage had to be an unofficial one; there was no proof that her first husband was dead. But despite this difficulty and the difference in their interests, their marriage lasted forty-five years. If Deborah occasionally lost her turbulent temper, Franklin was not bothered by these outbursts for long. A first child, William, arrived soon after they were married. Another boy, Francis, died at the age of four. And there was a daughter, Sarah—Franklin's beloved "Sally."

With Deborah to help, Franklin added a stationery store and a book store to his print shop. The combined enterprise seems to have sold anything on which a profit could be made. Franklin's mother-in-law made a medicinal ointment. Franklin's store handled it, as well as soap made by two of his brothers. Other items carried in the store at one time or another included chocolate, coffee, tea, linseed oil, Rhode Island cheese and codfish, compasses and scales, cloth, iron stoves, a fishing net, palm oil, and lottery tickets. Though later Franklin was to head an abolition society, at this time he even bought and sold indentured servants.

But Franklin's first love was his newspaper, which he had decided to start before his marriage. There was already a paper in Philadelphia, *The American Mercury*, published by Andrew Bradford, but it was boring. The town was ready, Franklin figured, for something more lively. Foolishly, he disclosed his plan to publish such a paper to one of Keimer's men who applied to him for a job, and the man ran back to Keimer with the secret. Franklin's former employer rushed into print with a paper of his own, which appeared on the day before Christmas, 1728, with the ambitious title, *The Universal Instructor in All Arts and Sciences: and Pennsylvania Gazette*. There was no room in Philadelphia for three papers, so Franklin determined to put Keimer's paper out of business.

He contributed a series of anony-

LIBRARY COMPANY OF PHILADELPHIA

Numb. XI.

THE

Pennſylvania *GAZETTE.*

Containing the freſheſt Advices Foreign and Domeſtick.

From Thurſday, September 25. to Thurſday, October 2. 1729.

THE Pennſylvania Gazette *being now to be carry'd on by other Hands, the Reader may expect ſome Account of the Method we deſign to proceed in.*

Upon a View of Chambers's *great Dictionaries, from whence were taken the Materials of the* Univerſal Inſtructor in all Arts and Sciences, *which uſually made the Firſt Part of this Paper, we find that beſides their containing many Things abſtruſe or inſignificant to us, it will probably be fifty Years before the Whole can be gone thro' in this Manner of Publication. There are likewiſe in thoſe Books continual References from Things under one Letter of the Alphabet to thoſe under another, which relate to the ſame S… and are neceſſary to explain a… theſe taken in their Turn m… Years di… deſi…*

There are many who have long deſired to ſee a good News-Paper in Pennſylvania; *and we hope thoſe Gentlemen who are able, will contribute towards the making This ſuch. We ask Aſſiſtance, becauſe we are fully ſenſible, that to publiſh a good News-Paper is not ſo eaſy an Undertaking as many People imagine it to be. The Aut…* a Gazette *(in the Opinion of the L… to be qualified with a… with Languages, a… of Writing and… telligibly, a… to ſpeak… acquai…*

Franklin is pictured here looking at a fresh issue of the newspaper he bought from his incompetent former employer, Keimer. A far better journalist, Franklin soon shortened Keimer's ponderous title to The Pennsylvania Gazette, *and vastly improved the paper's typography and design. In the first issue (above) he explained that he had also eliminated Keimer's serialization of an encyclopedia, "as it will probably be fifty Years before the Whole can be gone thro' in this Manner of Publication."*

mous articles in the form of letters to Bradford's paper. Franklin was one of the best writers in America at the time, and with his work running in the *Mercury*, few would read Keimer's *Gazette*. As with Silence Dogood, he pretended to be a woman. In the first letter he said, "Sometimes I propose to deliver lectures of morality or philosophy, and (because I am naturally inclined to be meddling with things that do not concern me) perhaps I may sometimes talk politics." He signed the letter "The Busy Body."

The Busy Body letters were an immediate success. In an interesting and humorous manner, they dealt with little incidents in the life of Philadelphia. At the time, there was a rumor that pirate gold was buried on the banks of the Delaware River, and many people were neglecting their work to dig for it. The Busy Body pointed out how foolish this was, and ended by telling a story about a farmer who gave his son a field, saying "I give thee now a valuable parcel of land; I assure thee that I have found a considerable quantity of gold by digging there; thee may'st do the same. But thee must carefully observe this; never dig more than plow deep."

At the end of six weeks, everybody was reading the *Mercury*; nobody was reading the *Gazette*. Poor Keimer sold his paper to Franklin very cheaply and went off to Barbados, in the West Indies, never knowing that Franklin was the busybody who had taken his subscribers away. Of course, Frank-

lin contributed no more to the *Mercury* as he began devoting his energies to his own paper. Under Franklin, the *Gazette* flourished. It remained one of the foremost early American newspapers until it died, under different ownership, in 1815.

Franklin, never resting, sought other printing ventures. In 1732, he was the publisher of the first foreign-language newspaper in the colonies, the *Philadelphische Zeitung*, aimed at the large German-speaking population in the region. This failed after a few issues. At about the same time, Franklin launched what was to become one of his greatest successes and sources of fame: an almanac. In colonial days there were usually only two pieces of printed matter in most homes, a Bible and an almanac. A printer might not make money on a newspaper or on books, but he was almost sure to make money on an almanac. At the age of twenty-six, Franklin decided to publish one.

While Franklin's most lasting fame as a writer grew out of this almanac, very little in it was original with him. Like all other almanacs, it was a paper-bound, pocket-size booklet which noted the holidays, the tides, the quarters of the moon, the dates of fairs and court sessions, and con-

The elegant, bewigged Franklin portrayed here was in his early forties when The Pennsylvania Gazette *and his other enterprises were flourishing. This is the first known of many Franklin portraits painted from life.*

BE MERRY AND WISE

Two of Franklin's main concerns during his days as a businessman were his print shop and the Junto, a group of young men who gathered weekly to discuss trade, politics, and philosophy, and to drink a little beer, as in the scene above from an English advertising card of the period. The old illustrations at right show three principal printing crafts: book binding (top), working the press, and type casting.

tained all kinds of tidbits of information. The name Franklin gave it, *Poor Richard's Almanack*, may have come from *Poor Robin's Almanack*, which his brother James was already publishing in New England. He even borrowed the name Richard from an English astrologer, Richard Saunders. What was original was Franklin's method of launching his almanac—with the first of his famous hoaxes.

Over the name of Richard Saunders, he wrote a preface to the first edition of the almanac, saying that he was a poor astrologer whose wife nagged him to stop gazing at the stars and go to work. He had long wanted to make some money by publishing an almanac, but withheld because his good friend, Titan Leeds, was in that business and he did not want to interfere with him. But now, said Saunders, the stars told him that Leeds was going to die on October 17, 1733, so there was no reason why he, Saunders, should not go into the almanac business. Actually, Titan Leeds was the editor of an almanac printed by Andrew Bradford. He immediately rushed into print to deny that he was going to die—he lived healthily through the

OVERLEAF: *For many years Franklin's print shop and home in Philadelphia was on lower Market Street, near a bustling intersection of trade and travel. This engraving shows the corner of Third and Market streets after the Revolution, when the city's architecture and the citizens' clothing were considerably more elaborate than in colonial times.*

45

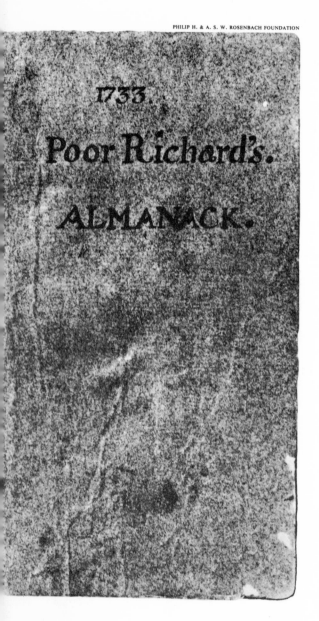

"fatal" date—and heaped all kinds of abuse on Franklin, who in turn must have basked delightedly in the publicity he had created for himself and his almanac.

Poor Richard's Almanack did come to differ in one decisive respect from other almanacs. "Observing that it was generally read," Franklin said, "I considered it a proper vehicle for conveying instruction among the common people, who bought scarcely any other books; I therefore filled all the little spaces that occurred between the remarkable days of the calendar with proverbial sentences." These proverbial sentences were the "Sayings of Poor Richard." Throughout the world people are familiar with some of them, and they are the only part of Franklin's writing that are generally known.

He gathered them from the literature of many ages and many nations, drawing on his self-taught knowledge of French, Spanish, Italian, German, and Latin to replenish the supply from year to year. It was not a matter of merely copying the sayings; he made them more pointed and more easily understandable. In their original form, most of these proverbs would long since have been forgotten. As Franklin revised them, many have lasted for centuries as part of our common speech. It is rather difficult, for instance, to understand the old proverb, "Fresh fish and new-come guests smell, but that they are three days old." Franklin's version is much

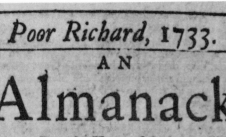

Poor Richard, 1733.

A N

Almanack

For the Year of Chrift

1733,

Being the Firft after LEAP YEAR:

And makes fince the Creation	Years
By the Account of the Eaftern *Greeks*	7241
By the Latin Church, when ☉ ent. ♈	6932
By the Computation of *W. W.*	5742
By the *Roman* Chronology	5682
By the *Jewifh* Rabbies	5494

Wherein is contained

The Lunations, Eclipfes, Judgment of the Weather, Spring Tides, Planets Motions & mutual Afpects, Sun and Moon's Rifing and Setting, Length of Days, Time of High Water, Fairs, Courts, and obfervable Days.

Fitted to the Latitude of Forty Degrees, and a Meridian of Five Hours Weft from *London*, but may without fenfible Error, ferve all the adjacent Places, even from *Newfoundland* to *South-Carolina*.

By *RICHARD SAUNDERS*, Philom.

PHILADELPHIA:

Printed and fold by B. *FRANKLIN*, at the New Printing-Office near the Market.

The Anatomy of Man's Body as govern'd by the Twelve Conftellations.

♈ The Head and Face.

♊ Arms
♌ Heart
♎ Reins
♐ Thighs
♒ Legs

♉ Neck
♋ Breaft
♍ Bowels
♏ Secrets
♑ Knees

♓ The Feet.

To know where the Sign is.

Firft Find the Day of the Month, and againft the Day you have the Sign or Place of the Moon in the 6th Column. Then finding the Sign here, it fhews the Part of the Body it governs.

The Names and Characters of the Seven Planets.

☉ Sol, ♄ Saturn, ♃ Jupiter, ♂ Mars, ♀ Venus, ☿ Mercury, ☽ Luna, ☊ Dragons Head and ☋ Tail.

The Five Afpects.

☌ Conjunction, ☍ Oppofition, ∗ Sextile.
△ Trine, □ Quartile.

The first issue of Poor Richard's Almanack *(whose cover and title page are shown opposite and above, left) quickly outsold rival almanacs for 1733. By 1760, the year in which the strange physiological explanations (above, right) appeared, the almanac was being widely read and imitated in the colonies and in England.*

49

more direct: "Fish and visitors stink in three days." Sometimes he changed only a word to make a proverb more meaningful. "Many strokes fell great oaks" became, under Franklin's editing, "Little strokes fell great oaks."

Much of the wisdom Franklin put in Poor Richard's mouth dealt with industry and frugality—the importance of working hard and saving money. After he had been publishing the almanac for twenty-five years, Franklin wove many of these proverbs into the preface of the almanac for 1757, and gained enduring international esteem for his own industry in doing so. The preface started with a story about a country auction at which all the people were complaining about high taxes while they waited for the goods to be placed on sale. Turning to a "plain, clean old man" who was standing by, they asked, "Pray, Father Abraham, what think you of the times? Will not these heavy taxes quite ruin the country? How shall we ever be able to pay them? What would you advise us to do?"

The old man then delivered a sermon in which he pointed out that the taxes laid on by the government were not nearly so heavy as taxes that people laid on themselves by wasting time and money and by buying things they did not need. "We are taxed twice as much by our idleness," he said, "three times as much by our pride, and four times as much by our folly." Throughout this speech appeared scores of proverbs that had appeared in the

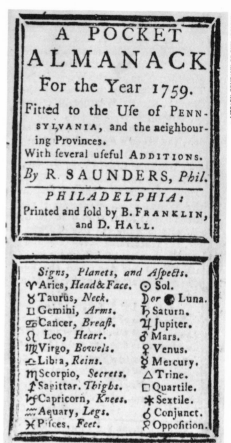

Above is the title page from the 1733 edition of Franklin's almanac. It lists Richard Saunders as the author; he was a fictitious character otherwise known as "Poor Richard." Astrology was an important ingredient in this and most other almanacs. The zodiac symbols in the center of each woodcut at right—from the 1749 edition—represent March, July, September, November, and December.

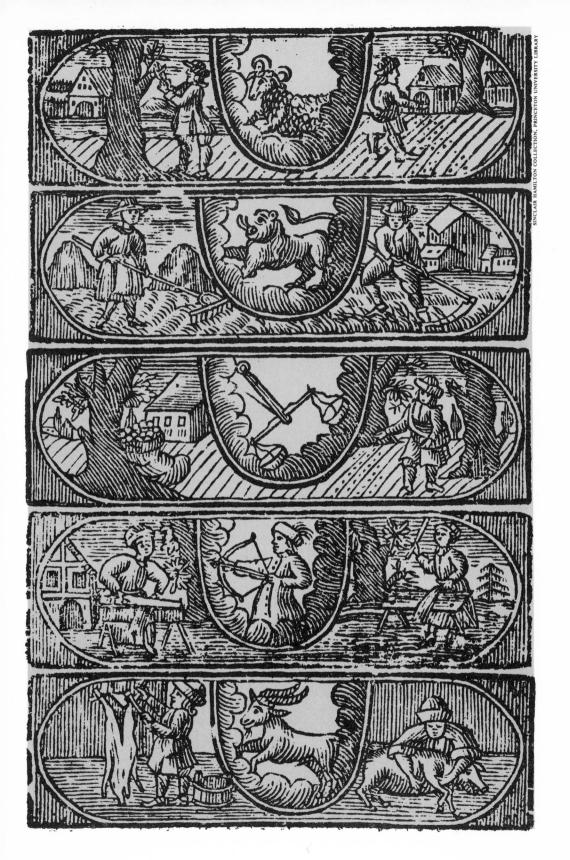

almanac in the previous quarter century, including:

"God helps them that help themselves."

"Up, Sluggard, and waste not life; in the grave will be sleeping enough."

"Early to bed and early to rise makes a man healthy, wealthy and wise."

"Constant dropping wears away stones."

"Beware of little expenses; a small leak will sink a great ship."

"A plowman on his legs is higher than a gentleman on his knees."

" 'Tis hard for an empty bag to stand upright."

"A word to the wise is enough."

The preface was an immediate success throughout the colonies, and later in England and France. It was soon published by itself under the title *The Way to Wealth*, and has been reprinted more often than any book but the Bible and a few others. There have been over 1,000 editions in English and about 300 in other languages. In Franklin's day, the French nobles and clergy distributed it widely among the people. The thrifty French took it very much to heart, and the creator of "Bonhomme Richard" became something of a hero to them—a reputation that was to help his country win its revolution decades later.

Franklin is pictured opposite in a richly furnished setting and gentlemanly clothing; he could well afford both at the prosperous midpoint of his life. The velvet-jacketed boy is probably meant to be his son William.

In 1748, twenty years after he had started the printing shop, Franklin became his own best evidence of the soundness of his advice; at the age of forty-two, he was able to retire from active business. He had set up several young men in business as printers and publishers in other colonies—New York, South Carolina, Connecticut, and the islands of Antigua and Jamaica. He received one-third of the profits from these enterprises. To a partner, whom he had taken on in Philadelphia, Ben now turned over his business there. From this transaction and his other resources he received over a thousand pounds a year, a sum equal to the salary of the governor of Pennsylvania.

"I am," Franklin wrote at the time, "in a fair way to having no other tasks than such as I shall like to give myself, and of enjoying what I look upon as a great happiness: leisure to read, study and make experiments, and converse . . . on such points as may produce something for the common benefits of mankind, uninterrupted by the little cares and fatigues of business." In this year of his "retirement," when Patrick Henry was only twelve and George Washington sixteen, Benjamin Franklin could not tell that he had as many years ahead of him as behind. During the coming years, he would be more active than ever, his energies and talents decisively affecting the momentous movements of science and history that were then under way.

3

Experiments and Inventions

When Benjamin Franklin decided, in 1748, to retire from business in order to "read, study, and make experiments," he was undoubtedly hoping to devote much of his time to the study of electricity, a little understood phenomenon that had come to fascinate him as he approached the midpoint of his life. Two years before, on a trip to Boston, he had met the engaging Dr. Archibald Spencer, a Scottish physician and lecturer on natural philosophy who used electrical experiments to illustrate his talks. Franklin saw some of these experiments, and his inquiring mind was immediately stimulated by them. "They were imperfectly performed," commented Franklin in his autobiography, "as he [Spencer] was not very expert; but being a subject quite new to me, they equally surprised and pleased me." Later that year, Spencer visited Philadelphia. Before he left, he had sold most of his experimental apparatus to an interested Franklin.

During the winter, Franklin the businessman-printer became more and more Franklin the scientist. Through Peter Collinson, a member of the Royal Society of London, he ordered still more equipment to supplement what he had bought from Spencer. His house on Market Street was, Franklin wrote, "continually full . . . with people who came to see these new wonders." By the following March, he was completely involved in the wonders himself, as he explained

This allegorical painting by Benjamin West dramatically depicts Franklin drawing electricity from the skies. By proving that electricity and lightning were identical, he gained enduring fame in the world of science.

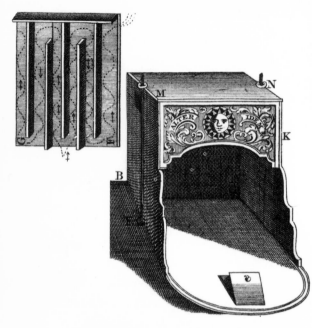

Among Franklin's inventions outside the field of electricity are the ingenious devices on these pages. At top left are bifocals designed by Franklin at the age of seventy-seven to allow him to see at different ranges with the same glasses. The top of the lens was ground for distant vision, the bottom for reading. At left is the Franklin stove and a cross-section of its air box. Below is the armonica, a musical instrument played by rubbing fingers against rotating hemispheres of glass. Mozart composed a solo adagio for the instrument. At top right is the mystery clock, so named because all its workings were hidden. Beneath it is an odometer. When attached to the axle of a wheel, it made a rough measure of a carriage's mileage. At bottom right is a combination chair and table—much like today's school chair—made from Franklin's design around 1800.

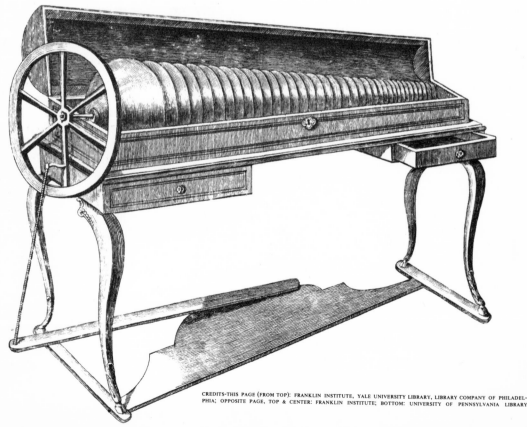

in a letter to Collinson. "I never was before engaged in any study that so totally engrossed my attention and my time as this has lately done," wrote Franklin, "for what with making experiments when I can be alone, and repeating them to my friends and acquaintances who, from the novelty of the thing, come continually in crowds to see them, I have during some months past had little leisure for anything else."

Franklin had always been an inventor of sorts, and his preoccupation with electricity had been preceded by a good deal of experimentation. While still a busy printer he built the "Pennsylvania Fire-place," known today as the Franklin stove. Open fireplaces allowed nearly all the heat to escape up the chimney and were often unbearably smoky. Franklin devised a false chimney back which kept smoke out of the room by forcing it up the flue created by the false back. Fresh air, warmed as it circulated up through the radiator-like air box, rushed out through side vents and quickly warmed the room.

Franklin tinkered with other ideas and thought up a number of new devices—bifocals, an odometer, and a musical instrument called an armonica, to name a few. Probably, he would have made a fortune by patenting any of them, but he refused to do so. "As we enjoy great advantages from the inventions of others," he wrote, "we should be glad of an opportunity to serve others by an inven-

tion of ours; and this we should do freely and generously."

Franklin long felt that ideas as well as inventions should be shared and had expounded this view in a pamphlet entitled *A Proposal for Prompting Useful Knowledge*, published in 1743. Franklin urged all men in the colonies who had the time and interest to investigate natural phenomena to exchange their findings through a central clearing house. Out of his proposal grew the American Philosophical Society, the country's first scientific association.

In addition to helping establish the society, Franklin throughout his life applied his fine analytical mind to problems in geology, meteorology,

By taking air and water temperatures on his transatlantic voyages, and utilizing information from other oceanographers, Franklin determined the course of the Gulf Stream. Above are Franklin's findings on detailed and large-scale charts of the current's flow.

physics, chemistry, astronomy, mathematics, aeronautics, navigation, agriculture, medicine, hygiene, seismology (the study of earthquakes), hydrography (the study of ocean currents), ethnology (the study of races of man), and paleontology (the study of fossils). Such was the intellectual breadth of the man who was fascinated by Dr. Spencer's demonstration.

In Franklin's time, electricity was a phenomenon little understood. It was veiled in superstition and had remained an obscure subject since classical times. In the sixth century B.C. a Greek philosopher named Thales had noticed that amber, when rubbed, attracted light objects such as feathers. Three hundred years later, another Greek, Theophrastus, observed that this was also true of certain gems when they were rubbed. Almost two thousand years passed before William Gilbert, physician to Queen Elizabeth, wrote a book on magnetism. In this work, those substances which became magnetically charged when rubbed were called "electrums" from the Latin word for amber. From Gilbert's new word the term "electricity" was derived.

By the 1740's it was known that electricity was more than just magnetism. A kind of generator had been invented, consisting of some globes or glass tubes that produced electrical charges when rubbed. European scientists had discovered that electricity could be transmitted through some things, like metal, but not through others, like wax or silk, and that it could be gathered in an insulated conductor such as a musket barrel hung by silk threads. They had learned that electrically charged substances sometimes attracted objects and sometimes repelled them depending, scientists thought, on the kind of material that was rubbed, and they believed two kinds of electricity were involved.

In 1745, shortly before Franklin met Spencer, a scientist named Pieter van Musschenbroek, who was working in Leyden, in the Netherlands, invented a specially designed device for storing an electrical charge—the first condenser. The Leyden jar, as his invention came to be called, was a foil-wrapped glass bottle, filled with water or metal shot, with a wire running down through its cork.

Still, no practical use was known for electricity. It was merely an interesting curiosity. Electricians had "acts" in which they pulled sparks from boys' ears and made their hair stand on end. A French electrician had amused Louis XV and his court by shocking seven hundred monks so that they all jumped into the air at once. But the possibility of harnessing this novelty into the great medium for transmitting power that it is today was probably beyond the imagination of anyone of Franklin's day. When the retired printer and a few other dedicated amateurs from the Junto and the Philosophical Society started a series of experiments in his home, it is unlikely that they had any particular vision in mind or any goal other than studying the effects of this strange new force.

Theirs were not elaborate experiments. They had only the simple apparatus of Dr. Spencer and a Leyden

OVERLEAF: *Franklin saw no immediate use for electricity, and during his lifetime it remained as much a novelty as a subject for scientific study. Here some Americans, about 1790, amuse themselves by rubbing rods to produce charges of static electricity.*

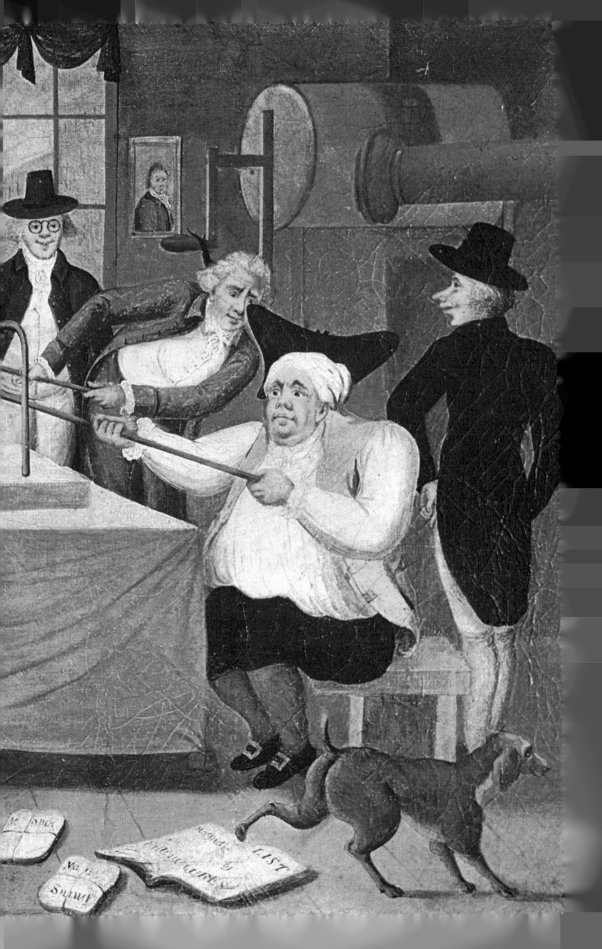

jar sent from England by Collinson. Most of their equipment they improvised from such simple things as a salt shaker, a vinegar bottle, a pump handle, and the gold inlay on the binding of a book. When they learned something new, Franklin wrote a simple description of the experiment. He said that if his scientific observations were not the truth they were at least as naked as truth, for he did not disguise them in Greek or clothe them in algebra. Most of his findings were given to the world through his letters to Collinson. The Englishman published the letters as pamphlets, and later assembled them into a book.

From an early experiment that Franklin had described in these letters came one of the most important findings ever made in the field of electricity, the discovery of positive and negative electricity. The amateur scientists gathered in Franklin's home, and Franklin selected three of the men, labeling them A, B, and C, to take part in an experiment. Franklin studied the spark that passed between the men as the electricity in their bodies was varied. From his observations he concluded that there were not two kinds of electricity, one that attracted and one that repelled—there was only one kind, but sometimes there might be more of it and sometimes there might be less. A man who had more electricity than his normal amount would be "electricized" *positively*, or would be said to have a *plus* charge. Conversely,

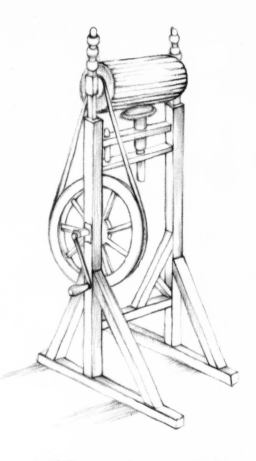

In 1747, an experimenter in Leyden, Holland, discovered the first reliable means of storing electricity. He found that the charge made by rubbing a revolving glass sphere could be maintained in a vessel half filled with water—as in the drawing at right. Connecting a number of improved Leyden jars together, Franklin devised a kind of storage battery (right, above). He also refined the glass rubbing technique for producing electricity. His generator (above) set up a charge when its glass roller was rotated against a wool pad.

62

DRAWINGS BY JOAN BERG

63

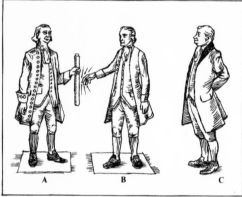

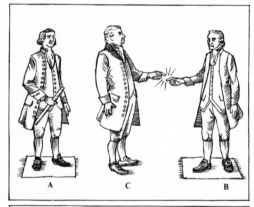

Describing his discovery of negative and positive electricity, Franklin wrote about the electrical interaction of three subjects, as seen in these drawings. In the first panel, A and B are insulated by the waxed squares on which they stand. C is uninsulated. At the beginning of the experiment all three men have their normal amount of electricity.

A, by rubbing a glass tube, has transferred some of his own electricity to the tube. When B puts his hand toward the tube, a spark jumps between it and his knuckle, as in the second panel. With that spark, B picks up from the tube some of the electricity that A has lost, thereby becoming charged with more electricity than normal, while A has less than normal.

Next C, with his normal supply of electricity, puts his knuckle toward the supercharged B, as in the third panel. C gets a spark, representing the flow of electricity which B received from the now undercharged A.

If neither A nor B makes contact with C, then a much greater spark will jump between the two of them (last panel). This is because the difference in the amount of electricity in A and B is greater than between either of them and C. "Hence," wrote Franklin, "have arisen some new terms among us; we say that B is electricized positively: A negatively. Or rather, B is electricized plus and A minus." Thus, Franklin described one of the fundamental characteristics of electricity.

someone with less than his normal amount of electricity would be electricized *negatively*, or have a *minus* charge. This knowledge of positive and negative electricity was a step forward, and Franklin was starting to build the vocabulary of electricity as he laid the groundwork of the science.

In another experiment—attempting to analyze the Leyden jar—he soon realized that electricity could be stored more efficiently. Franklin described how he and his friends took "eleven panes of large sash-glass, armed with thin leaden plates pasted on each side, placed vertically and supported at two inches distance on silk cords, with hooks of thick leaden wire, one from each side . . . and convenient communications of wire and chain from the giving side of one pane to the receiving side of the other, so that the whole might be charged together with the same labor as one single pane." Franklin called this device by a new name, an "electrical battery." It was the world's first.

Franklin and his fellow researchers, in another test, placed an iron ball about three inches in diameter on top of a bottle. They hung a cork ball about an inch in diameter from the ceiling on a fine silk thread directly over the bottle so that the cork ball rested against the side of the iron ball. When the iron ball was electrified from a battery or Leyden jar, the cork ball bounced away from the iron ball about five or six inches. Then Franklin took a long, sharp bodkin—a large

Franklin made and used the crude generator above. By revolving the glass globe against a piece of chamois skin, a charge of static electricity was built up in the globe. The charge was drawn off by knitting needle tips and stored in Leyden jar batteries.

Like most representations of Franklin's kite experiment, this 1830 painting from a fire wagon panel is thoroughly inaccurate. Franklin, at forty-six, was not a gray-haired old man, and the boy with him was his son William, who was actually twenty-one at the time.

needle—and brought it slowly toward the iron ball. When the bodkin reached a point about six or eight inches from the iron ball, the cork ball flew back. Obviously, the needle was drawing the electricity from the iron ball so that the cork ball was no longer repelled.

When Franklin repeated the experiment using a blunt rod instead of a pointed bodkin, he had to bring it to within an inch of the iron ball before the cork ball flew back. This indicated that a pointed object would draw off electricity more easily than a blunt one.

From such observations Franklin developed what he called the "doctrine of points." A short time later he wrote to Collinson saying, "The doctrine of points is very curious . . . I am of the opinion that houses, ships and even towers and churches may be effectually secured from the stroke of lightning by their means; for if, instead of the round balls of wood or metal which are commonly placed on the tops of the weathercocks, vanes or spindles of churches, spires and masts, there should be a rod of iron eight or ten feet in length, sharpened gradually to a point like a needle . . . the electrical fire would, I think, be drawn out of a cloud silently before it could come near enough to strike."

Luckily, nobody tried to build a lightning rod from this first description of Franklin's—he had neglected to ground the rod. Later he added the important provision of "a wire down the outside of a building into

Duc de Chaulnes.

The dangerous kite experiment was carried out by several Europeans, once even before Franklin made the proposed test himself. Above, in an engraving Franklin gave to the Philosophical Society, is a safe-guarded version of the test by the Duc de Chaulnes, a French scientist. He sits suspended and insulated from the ground, a protective light-ning rod overhead, handling his kite through a remote-controlled winch.

the ground, or down one of the shrouds of a ship until it reaches the water." The lightning rod, for a long time called the Franklin rod, was complete.

Still, Franklin had not yet proved that lightning and electricity were identical. Legend has it that he did this by flying a kite in a thunderstorm. Actually, that is not the way in which the identity was first proved, and Franklin was not the first to prove it.

In 1750 Franklin wrote to Collinson outlining an experiment which would prove that lightning was electrical. He proposed to build a sentry box on the top of a tall tower or steeple, with a pointed rod running out the door and up above the sentry box for twenty or thirty feet. A man was to step on an "electrical stand" (an insulated platform) inside the box. "If the electrical stand be kept clean and dry," Franklin said, "a man standing on it . . . might be electrified and afford sparks." (He was thinking of giving the man a positive electrical charge.) Franklin never went through with this dangerous but crucial test. He was waiting for the steeple of Christ Church in Philadelphia to be built in order to try it, and the steeple was not finished for some years.

Before that, in 1751, Collinson published Franklin's letters on electricity and other subjects—the first of many collections of Franklin's writings. The book was translated into French. And in a suburb of Paris, a French scientist named D'Alibard read the

The American closest to Franklin in scientific stature was David Rittenhouse (above). He succeeded Franklin as head of the American Philosophical Society; built America's first telescope; and did important research in electricity, magnetism, and mathematics.

translation and wanted to try the experiment, but there was no tall spire or steeple. So he erected a pointed rod forty feet high on a plank resting on three glass bottles for insulators. He waited for a thunderstorm, but he was not present when the storm broke. When the lightning flashed, a former dragoon who was guarding the apparatus ran to the base of the rod with a Leyden jar. Lightning crackled blue and white around the rod as he held the jar near. The jar was instantly charged, thus proving the identity of lightning with electricity.

But what of the famous kite that Franklin is supposed to have flown? Franklin never said that he did or did not make the kite experiment. He did describe how it could be made by fastening a sharp-pointed wire about a foot long to the top of the upright stick of a kite. "To the end of the twine, next the hand, is to be tied a silk ribbon, and where the silk and twine join, a key may be fastened. The kite is to be raised when a thunder-gust appears to be coming on, and the person who holds the string must stand within a door or window or under some cover, so that the silk ribbon may not be wet . . . As soon as any of the thunderclouds come over the kite, the pointed wire will draw the electric fire from them . . . and when the rain has wet the kite and twine so that it can conduct the electric fire freely, you will find it stream out plentifully from the key at the approach of your knuckles."

Franklin communicated his observations on electrical phenomena to the Englishman Peter Collinson (above), a Quaker merchant and member of the Royal Society. Franklin had corresponded with him for twenty-five years before they met in London in 1757.

71

The only account of Franklin having made such a test himself is in a book by the Englishman Joseph Priestley, written fifteen years after the alleged date of Franklin's experiment. Priestley, a scientist himself, said Franklin made the experiment with his son William in June of 1752, "a month after the electricians in France had verified the same theory, but before he heard of anything they had done." Since Franklin saw Priestley's manuscript before it was published, it probably was an accurate account of an actual event.

In his study of electricity Franklin did not always approach the phenomenon with solemn scientific seriousness. On one occasion he installed what might be the first electrical appliance in an American home. He ran a wire from a lightning rod through a glass tube in his roof down to a point outside his study. Here he divided the wire and connected the ends to two bells about six inches apart. Between the bells he hung a brass ball on a silk thread. When the rod attracted lightning, the ball then bounced back and forth, ringing the bells. Then Franklin would connect batteries, or Leyden jars, to the wires and charge them—a much easier way of getting electricity than rubbing a glass tube.

One night the apparatus did not work quite as he expected. He had been sleeping and was awakened "by loud cracks on the staircase . . . Starting up and opening the door, I perceived that the brass ball, instead of

In 1754 a scientist in Russia was electrocuted while attempting to perform Franklin's kite experiment. He had neither grounded his equipment nor insulated himself, and so received the full force of a lightning discharge.
N.Y. PUBLIC LIBRARY

vibrating as usual between the bells, was repelled and kept at a distance from both, while the fire passed, sometimes in very large, quick cracks from bell to bell, and sometimes in a continued dense white stream, seemingly as large as my finger, whereby the whole staircase was inlighted as with sunshine, so that one might see to pick up a pin." Once when Franklin was away, his wife Deborah, who found the bell apparatus unnerving, had it quietly removed. In this she was infinitely wiser than her shrewd husband, for the apparatus was certainly not a safe thing to have around the house.

Franklin apparently did not realize that many of his electrical experiments were dangerous. A scientist in Russia was killed trying to duplicate the lightning test designed by the Frenchman D'Alibard. Franklin's kite experiment might have been fatal had a strong bolt been attracted. In fact, Franklin came very close to electrocuting himself in a minor experiment that had to do with his recurring concern for good food. He thought that meat might be more tender if the animal from which it came was killed by electricity. Two days before Christmas, 1750, he hooked up several very large electrified jars. Then, while trying to apply the current to a turkey, he touched the positive and negative terminals.

He said that others who were present told him that there was a great flash and a crack as loud as a pistol, "though I neither saw one or heard the other . . . I then felt what I know not well how to describe; a universal blow throughout my whole body from head to foot, which seemed within as well as without; after which the first thing I took notice of was a violent shaking of my whole body." Franklin survived the experience with no serious consequences.

A supreme bit of electrical nonsense was described by Franklin in a letter to Collinson in 1749. He proposed an electrical banquet, which may or may not have occurred. In it Franklin and his friends were to light glasses of brandy with a spark from an electric current sent across the Schuylkill River through the water. They were to kill a turkey with an electric shock and roast it on an "electrical jack" over a fire lighted by an electrified bottle. They would then drink toasts to "all the famous electricians in England, France and Germany" from "electrified bumpers" while guns were electrically discharged. Franklin described an electrified bumper as "a small thin glass tumbler, near filled with wine and electrified. This when brought to the lips, gives a shock if the party be close shaved, and does not breathe on the liquor."

Throughout his experiments, Franklin always gave full credit to his fellow experimenters. But it was obvious that he was the prime force and the guiding genius, and unsought honors were heaped upon him. In 1753 Harvard and Yale, and later William and Mary, conferred on him the honorary degree of Master of Arts. The Royal Society of London made him a member and awarded him a gold medal. The king of France sent his commendations. In the 1750's the self-taught Franklin was known throughout Europe as America's leading scientist. In time, however, he would achieve still greater fame as America's leading diplomat.

4

"General" Franklin

In 1751, Collinson received a letter in London authorizing him to spend up to three hundred pounds for fees and charges—whatever had to be paid to obtain an appointment for Franklin as postmaster general of the colonies. The less the appointment cost, the better, Franklin told him and quipped, " 'tis an office for life only, which is a very uncertain tenure."

Collinson was only half successful in getting Franklin what he wanted. In 1753, after the death of the previous postmaster, Franklin was named to the position jointly with William Hunter of Virginia. As deputy post-

In his public career, Franklin started and joined many organizations. At left he is wearing a helmet of the Union Fire Company, which he formed; the company's Philadelphia engine house is in the background.

masters general, they were to be in charge of the northern and southern colonies' postal systems, respectively. In addition, Franklin was to be comptroller (chief financial officer) for the entire colonial service.

In seeking the office, Franklin had violated a rule of his: "Never ask, never refuse, nor ever resign." But the establishment of Philadelphia as the center of the colonial postal system would mean prestige for the city, just as the crown appointment would mean honor for Franklin. He was allotted three hundred pounds to run the department, and was permitted to keep any profits over that amount. There had never been any profits for the colonial postal system, but Franklin was confident that he would earn his fee, and more.

Before he took on the joint postmastership, the versatile Philadelphian already had demonstrated that he was a conscientious public servant. He had organized Philadelphia's first fire department and reorganized its first police force—the city watch. He had served on the City Council as an alderman, and was a member of the Pennsylvania Assembly. He was already Philadelphia's postmaster.

Along the way, his ever-active pen had led to the creation of the Academy of Philadelphia in 1751. This later became the University of Pennsylvania. Franklin had been distressed that his colony had no college. Massachusetts had Harvard; Connecticut had Yale; Virginia had William and Mary; and New Jersey had a college that would later become Princeton. But, in Pennsylvania, there was no seat of higher education. So, in 1749, Franklin wrote *Proposals Relating to the Education of Youth in Pennsylvania,* which called for such an institution, and later that same year a group of prominent Pennsylvanians began to plan for an academy. Franklin, who had less than two years of formal schooling, was chosen the first president of the academy's Board of Trustees, a position he held until 1756.

He also helped organize and finance the first free hospital in the colonies, and was one of twelve Philadelphians who set up the first fire insurance company in 1752. But one of the most notable accomplishments of these years had occurred in 1747, the year before he retired from business and

About 1736, Franklin proposed reorganizing Philadelphia's city watch, which, he said, was often staffed by "ragamuffins." A well-disciplined police force, together with street lighting, was later voted; and ladder-toting lamplighters, like the one in the drawing above, were soon making regular rounds at twilight.

six years before he was named deputy postmaster general.

France and Spain were at war with England in Europe, and the six-year-long struggle had quickly spread to the New World as well. Pennsylvania had little interest in the war until French and Spanish privateers sailed up the Delaware River and sacked two plantations a few miles below Philadelphia. Then it became frighteningly apparent to some that the city was wide open to attack by warships or privateers. In fact, there was no military organization at all in the city or province.

The Provincial Assembly was controlled by the Quakers, who were opposed to fighting—even in self-defense—and they would not vote money for arms. The wealthy merchants in Philadelphia would not spend money to defend the Quakers' property along with their own. Franklin said the merchants reminded him of a man "who refused to pump on a sinking ship because one on board whom he hated would be saved by it as well as himself."

Alarmed by this inaction, he wrote and printed a pamphlet entitled *Plain Truth*, which described what would happen if enemy warships attacked

Franklin is depicted as an energetic fire-fighter in this painting, which decorated a hand-powered water pump. The first fire company organized by Franklin was a volunteer group of thirty men who had meetings once a month and brought their own buckets.

the city. The rich, he said, "will flee through fear of torture . . . The man that has a wife and children will find them hanging on his neck, beseeching him with tears to quit the city and save his life . . . The few that remain will be unable to resist. Sacking the city will be the first, and burning it . . . the last act of the enemy."

After he had drawn a lurid picture of the city in flames, with people running and screaming through the streets, being hacked down by the ruthless privateersmen, he pointed out that there were certainly enough people to defend the colony. There were, he wrote, "60,000 fighting men, acquainted with firearms, many of them hunters and marksmen, hardy and bold. All we want is order, discipline and a few cannon. At present we are like the separate filaments of flax before the thread is formed . . . But *Union* would make us strong."

Franklin, ignoring the ineffectual Assembly, called several meetings to form a voluntary association for self-defense. In a roomy sail loft he met with nearly a hundred Philadelphia tradesmen and mechanics. They endorsed his plan for union, and he then presented it to some "principal gentlemen," mostly merchants, in the more fashionable surroundings of Roberts' Coffee House. When they too supported Franklin, he called a mass meeting for the following night. The gathering, held in one of Philadelphia's larger buildings, was well attended. Franklin read his pamphlet

This woodcut appeared in Franklin's pamphlet Plain Truth, *in which he urged the citizens of Pennsylvania to prepare defenses. Illustrating an ancient myth, it shows a horse-drawn wagon stuck in the mud; the wagoner prays to a heavenly Hercules for help. The moral of the fable is suggested by the Latin words* Non Votis—*Be not deceived.*

To protect Philadelphia, Franklin's Association constructed a battery (above) at a strategic defense point on the Delaware River. Franklin stood guard there in the summer of 1747.

and asked every man present to join the newly organized militia companies. More than five hundred men signed up then and there. Afterward, the idea of defense associations spread throughout Philadelphia, and eventually over ten thousand enrolled in association regiments. The Philadelphia regiment wanted to elect Franklin colonel, but since he had little military knowledge, he declined.

In the spring of 1748, he went to New York to try to borrow some cannon for the militia, but was refused at first by the royal governor, George Clinton. Franklin dined with Clinton, and during the course of the meal noticed that the governor was drinking wine quite heavily. After His Excellency had downed a few more glasses, Franklin again asked for the cannon. The governor offered six. Franklin suggested that he have some more wine. Before dinner was over, the mellowed governor had promised him eighteen guns which, their pleased recipient later noted, "we soon transported and mounted on our battery, where the Associators kept a nightly guard while the war lasted." He added, with obvious pride in his modest role, that "amongst the rest I regularly took my turn of duty as a common soldier." But the war bypassed Philadelphia, and in 1748 a peace treaty between England and France was signed.

By 1753, when he was appointed deputy postmaster general, Franklin the printer, publisher, politician, and promoter of public projects was highly respected throughout Pennsylvania. In the rest of the colonies, though, he was barely known. Still, if the public did not know of him, he had their welfare very much in mind. His position as postmaster led him to think naturally in terms of the colonies as a whole, for the postal service spanned them all. And his travels in the job both strengthened and helped him spread his ideas of unity among the colonial governments.

At the start of his postmastership, however, Franklin was primarily concerned with the practical aspects of the postal system's operation. He put the service on a paying basis for the crown, and he also made it a source of revenue for his family. He appointed his son William as comptroller of the northern postal system. His brother Peter Franklin came from Boston to be postmaster of Philadelphia, and another brother John Franklin filled a like post in Boston.

In the process of making the postal service financially sound, Franklin gave the colonies their first regular mail deliveries. He visited all the offices in the northern colonies and in Virginia and Maryland to install an improved accounting system, to establish new routes and more frequent service, and to select roads, fords, and ferries for the couriers. In Philadelphia he instituted the "penny post," whereby people who wanted their letters delivered might obtain the service for this extra fee.

When Franklin was postmaster of Philadelphia, he and other publishers had their newspapers carried free by the postal riders. Now, as deputy postmaster general, he ruled that all papers, including his own, had to pay postage. The post office was soon making money, but more important, the improved postal service became an efficient, practical means of drawing the scattered colonies together. Previously, the mails had been so undependable that people in different colonies seldom tried to communicate with each other by post, and messages sent by private means were even less reliable.

The colonies had always functioned as separate entities, carefully guarding their individual rights and powers. But the hope that they might work together, on some matters at least, had been brewing in Franklin's mind for some time. In 1751 he had outlined a plan to unify the colonies for defense against the Indians. But Franklin was unwilling to present his plan to the assemblies through their respective governors. He knew that crown-appointed officials were seldom trusted by the elected American assemblymen.

Instead, Franklin suggested they "pick out half a dozen men of good

Ignoring the regular postal service (and the God Mercury who wings overhead), a sea captain delivers a private letter in the 1748 almanac drawing at right. By instituting more efficient, business-like methods, Franklin increased the revenue of the postal service.

1748.

83

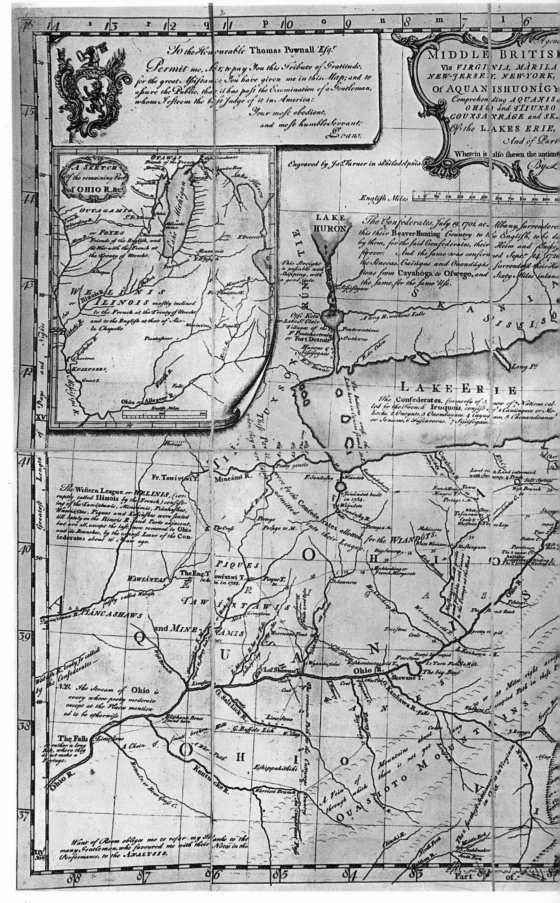

This map of the "Middle British Colonies in America," printed by Franklin in 1755, was co

...dered accurate enough to be generally accepted as the authority in settling boundary disputes.

JOIN, or DIE.

Indian tribes, often inflamed by the French, became an increasing threat to the British colonies in the 1750's. After going to sign a peace treaty with some of the Ohio tribes in 1753, Franklin observed that rum was also behind much Indian unrest—a point amply illustrated (below) in an early biography of Franklin. Later, in the first political cartoon to appear in an American newspaper (left), Franklin warned colonists to unite or risk being overrun.

understanding and address, and furnish them with a reasonable scheme and proper instructions and send them in the nature of ambassadors to other colonies, where they might apply particularly to all the leading men and by proper management get them to engage in promoting the scheme."

Franklin later compared the unorganized colonies with the federation of Indian tribes called the Six Nations, writing, "It would be a strange thing if six nations of ignorant savages should be capable of forming a scheme for such a union, and be able to execute it in such a manner that it has subsisted ages . . . and yet that a like union should be impractical for ten or a dozen English colonies to whom it is more necessary."

In 1754 Franklin again urged the adoption of his plan for union when representatives of six colonies met in Albany to discuss defense. Franklin was one of Pennsylvania's delegates. The conference, a landmark in pre-Revolutionary history, marked the first time so many colonies had conferred on the possibility of unified action.

During the talks, Franklin presented an essay, *Short Hints towards a Scheme for Uniting the Northern Colonies*, which repeated many of his ideas from the 1751 plan. His proposed union would deal not only with defense against the Indians, but would equip vessels to protect the coast from privateers and lend support to new settlements inland. The union would

BRITISH MUSEUM

After war erupted in Europe between Britain and France, the British moved troops into Pennsylvania to fight the French and their Indian allies. Pictured above, at right, are barracks in Philadelphia in 1758, and above, a soldier of a British regiment raised in America for the French and Indian war.

be headed by a military governor general appointed by the crown and supported by a tax on liquor or by stamps on legal documents. Franklin urged that the union originate with the colonies themselves, and not be imposed by England's distant Parliament, in which they were not represented.

After two weeks of discussion, the conference adopted a "Plan of Union" based primarily on Franklin's proposal. But the plan was never endorsed by the colonial assemblies. These local governments were too jealous of their prerogatives and too

suspicious of their neighbors to give up any of their authority to a central body. Franklin was distressed; later he would write, "I am still of the opinion that it would have been happy for both sides of the water if the plan of union had been adopted. The colonies, so united, would have been sufficiently strong to have defended themselves; there would have been no need of troops from England; of course, the subsequent pretense of taxing America and the bloody contest it occasioned would have been avoided. But such mistakes are not new; history is full of the errors of states and princes."

At Albany, Franklin met Massachusetts' staunchly royalist governor, William Shirley, who had a far different plan for union. He favored a council appointed by the crown, and taxes for defense levied on the colonies by Parliament. In three letters to Shirley, Franklin objected to this plan, anticipating some of the causes of the Revolution nearly twenty years before the first shot was fired. The people of the colonies, he wrote, would not be content to pay taxes imposed by a

Parliament in which they had no representation. "To propose taxing them by Parliament, and refuse them the liberty of choosing a representative council to meet in the colonies . . . shows a suspicion of their common sense and understanding."

Also, he said, British regulations then governing colonial trade were unfair. "Some manufactures we could make but are forbidden and must take them from British merchants; the whole price of these is a tax paid to Britain." These ideas—"taxation without representation" and "restraint of trade"—would become the battle cries of the Revolution.

As part of his plan for union, Franklin had also suggested the establishment of new colonies west of the Appalachians, to be settled jointly by existing colonies. The growing population of America would, he thought, move westward, develop new land, produce more, and consume more, and everybody would be better off if Americans were allowed to do this without restrictive trade laws.

It was typical of Franklin's farsightedness that he visualized the future of America in terms of the development of the West. Later, he tried to get charters for two colonies on land that is now Ohio and Indiana, but the attempt was sidetracked in the chaos of the Revolution. Franklin's sentiments, however, did not go unappreciated. The first territory west of the Appalachians was called Franklin until it was renamed Tennessee.

Soon after the Albany conference, most of Franklin's attention was required for narrower but more urgent concerns than those of union. The French and Indian War had erupted just before the conference. As the colonial representatives debated, Colonel George Washington was forced to surrender Fort Necessity after an overwhelming French attack. The war later came within seventy-five miles of Philadelphia when, on November 24, 1754, Shawnee Indians attacked the Pennsylvania village of Gnadenhuetten, killing many inhabitants and burning the settlement to the ground. The village was never rebuilt; today, the towns of Lehighton and Weissport are near its site.

Gnadenhuetten had been one of several communities in the area founded by German Moravians. This was a religious sect that practiced communal living. Franklin learned that they occasionally determined marriages by lot, and remarked that "if the matches were not made by the mutual choice of the parties, some of them may chance to be very unhappy. 'And so they may,' answered my informer, 'if you let the parties choose for themselves': which indeed, I could not deny."

A view of the carefully cultivated farm land east of Gnadenhuetten appears right, seen at the time of Franklin's expedition to Pennsylvania's frontier territories. The village was on the route of any attack on Philadelphia by the French and Indians to the west.

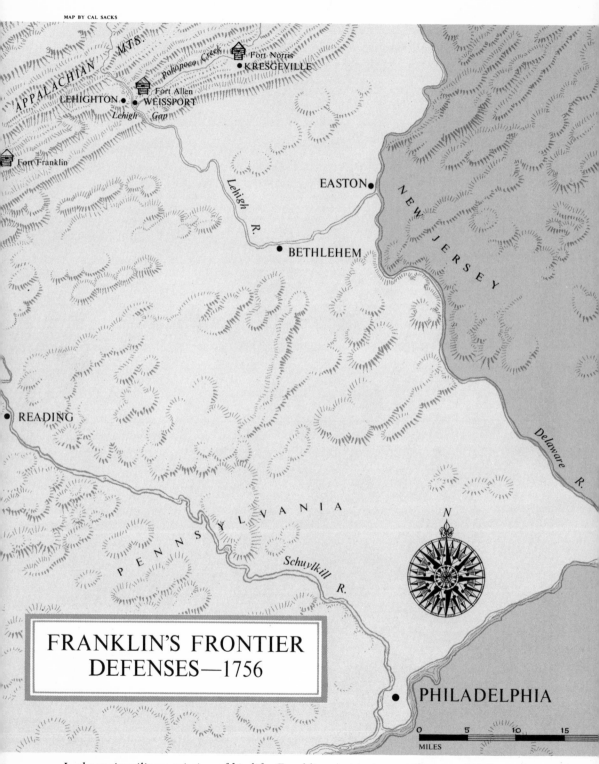

APPALACHIAN MTS.

Pohopoco Creek

Fort Norris
KRESGEVILLE

Fort Allen
LEHIGHTON • • WEISSPORT

Lehigh Gap

Fort Franklin

Lehigh R.

EASTON •

NEW JERSEY

• BETHLEHEM

• READING

Delaware R.

P E N N S Y L V A N I A

Schuylkill R.

N

FRANKLIN'S FRONTIER
DEFENSES—1756

• PHILADELPHIA

0   5   10   15

MILES

In the main military mission of his life, Franklin went to inspect threatened defenses in Bethlehem, Easton, and Reading, and then to the razed site of Gnadenhuetten, near the towns of Lehighton and Weissport. There he built Fort Allen in the strategic Lehigh Gap, after which he constructed forts Norris and Franklin in the Appalachian foothills.

Franklin saw the only active military service of his life when, in response to the Shawnee attack, Governor Robert Morris sent him and two other prominent Pennsylvanians to Bethlehem to arrange the defenses of the northwest frontier. Bethlehem, the principal Moravian settlement, was located near the Lehigh Gap, the only pass through the Appalachian Mountains from the northwest. In Bethlehem, the bishop of the Moravians insisted on calling the man who became the obvious leader of the expedition "General" Franklin. Upon inspection of the town, the "general" found that the Moravians had taken some steps to defend themselves, including the quaint precaution of placing "quantities of small paving stones between the windows of their high stone houses, for their women to throw down upon the head of any Indians. . . ."

Franklin understood the military situation: if the Indians got through Lehigh Gap, the German settlements in Pennsylvania's frontier regions

The Moravians, a Christian pacifist sect from Germany, were gentle people and ardent missionaries. Below, these pious settlers are baptizing three Indians as other Indian converts look on. The sect practiced a form of communal living. Franklin noted, "I found they worked for a common stock, ate at common tables, and slept in common dormitories."

HOLLEY, *Life of Benjamin Franklin*, 1848

*On his return from the frontier, Franklin was enthusi-
astically elected colonel of the Philadelphia militia
and unenthusiastically participated in a parade in his
honor (above). "I who am . . . above all things averse
to making show . . . suffered . . . much more pain than I
enjoyed pleasure," he wrote about such a procession.*

would be at their mercy. Worse, if the French followed, Philadelphia itself would be endangered. Or, if the French fortified the gap, one of the best routes to the West would be denied the English.

Gnadenhuetten, situated north of Bethlehem, squarely in front of the gap, was of obvious strategic importance. A detachment of soldiers had, in fact, already been sent out to hold the razed village. This was the situation when, having inspected Bethlehem, Franklin and his fellow defense commissioners met with Governor Morris in Reading. Then, on January 3, a runner brought news that the soldiers at Gnadenhuetten had been driven off by a surprise Indian attack. The governor and the commissioners decided that someone had to go to Gnadenhuetten immediately to supervise the construction of a fort at that strategic location. Franklin was elected.

He had never built a fort, but he had read a book, which still exists with his marginal notes, entitled *Short Treatise on Fortifications and Geometry.* He figured out how to build a log stockade, and with the help of a company of axemen, put one up. In spite of bad weather, the construction took only six days. Franklin then supervised the building of two forts east and west of Gnadenhuetten.

Throughout the expedition, Franklin, heavyset now and just turned fifty, endured the discomforts of rainy weather, rough quarters, and bad food without complaint. The "general" also discovered, that in addition to supervising the construction of the forts, he had five hundred men in his charge as well as uncounted refugees from the frontier settlements.

On February 1, after nearly a month of rugged frontier living, Franklin received word that Morris had called a special session of the Assembly for February 3. Turning over his command to a New England colonel, he hurried back to his civilian occupations. But his military days were not quite over. Back in Philadelphia, Franklin found that he had been appointed a colonel in charge of the city's militia, supported by regular British troops. This time, he accepted the honor although he soon questioned his wisdom in doing so. At least one immediate regret resulted from the appointment. "The first time I reviewed my regiment," he later wrote, "they accompanied me to my house, and would salute me with some rounds fired before my door, which shook down and broke several glasses of my electrical apparatus."

As he picked up the pieces, he might as well have packed all the equipment safely away; he would seldom use it again. His deepening involvement in the ever more complex affairs of colonial government meant the end of the leisurely life of scientific study to which he had once hoped to retire. For the next thirty years, "philosophy" would be only a spare-time pursuit of the busy statesman.

5

American in London

Alexander Wedderburn, the crown's most venomous lawyer, glowered for the benefit of his audience in the chamber of His Majesty's Privy Council. Thirty-six members of the noble council, sitting as the Lords Committee for Plantation Affairs, were at a long table. The Archbishop of Canterbury was among them. Eight earls were there, plus nine other peers. Standing behind the councilors was a throng of spectators, including many members of Parliament who had crowded into the room that January 29, 1774, to see England's major political event of the day.

As the main spokesman for America in London, Franklin bore the brunt of English resentment against the restless colonists. He is shown (standing, left) in the Privy Council hearing in which he was mercilessly derided.

Pointing dramatically to Benjamin Franklin, who was standing beside the chamber's fireplace wearing a velvet coat, Wedderburn thundered, "I hope, my Lords, you will mark and brand this man for the honor of this country, of Europe, and of mankind . . . He has forfeited all the respect of societies and men." The impassioned lawyer continued for almost an hour with a string of vicious accusations against the American who was, he said, "the first mover and prime conductor . . . the actor and secret spring . . . the inventor and first planner" of all the trouble between England and the American colonies, and who, with his friends, wished to erect "a tyranny greater than the Roman."

Franklin remained silent and expressionless throughout the denunciation. Supposedly he was there to petition the committee to remove the governor of Massachusetts. Officially it was not Franklin who was on trial. But all those present knew that the true purpose of the hearing was to discredit the famous American.

Such was the sorry climax of the years that Franklin had spent in England between 1757 and 1775. Originally he had been sent there by the Pennsylvania Assembly to smooth out the colony's differences with William Penn's sons, Thomas and Rich-

Richard Penn (above) and his brother Thomas, the "True and Absolute Proprietaries" of Pennsylvania, saw Franklin as a menace to their many financial interests.

ard, the proprietors of the colony. Unfortunately, the younger Penns cared little for the religious freedom that had motivated their father to found the colony, nor did they share his concern for the colonists' welfare. To them Pennsylvania was little more than a distant piece of real estate from which they wanted to earn the best possible income. By the middle 1750's their attitude had stirred up widespread resentment in the colony, and the Assembly wanted the right to tax the Penns' colonial holdings.

Early in 1757 the Assembly decided to send someone to London to plead their case with the brothers. Franklin was the man most trusted and most respected by the rival factions in the Assembly—the Quakers, the frontier farmers, the tradesmen, and the rich merchants. So, thirty-three years after his first arrival in the English capital, Benjamin Franklin found himself once again riding into London—on a venture that was to affect the course of his life decisively.

The mission, however, was doomed to failure. The Penns were suspicious of the Assembly in general and of Franklin in particular. His role in forming the colony's militia and his leadership of the Philadelphia regiment made them jealous of his popularity and apparent power. They snubbed Franklin by dealing with the Assembly only through the governor of the colony. This left Franklin little to do in his official capacity as a colonial agent. But as he made friends among important Englishmen, he found himself becoming more and more the unofficial spokesman for America.

He went home to Philadelphia in 1762, but in two years returned to London, with a petition from the Pennsylvania Assembly asking the king to dispossess the Penns of the province and make it a crown colony. The petition was ignored by the king's ministers and was in fact soon overshadowed in Franklin's own mind by a greater American problem. He found himself embroiled in the piece of legislation called the Stamp Act, which was passed by Parliament in February, 1765. The act increased the colonial tax load by requiring that stamps be placed on various legal papers, documents, and printed matter. For example, the stamp for a college diploma would cost ten pounds; for a liquor license, four pounds; for a pack of cards, one shilling; for an almanac, twopence; and so on for fifty-five items.

Franklin opposed the passage of the act, although he did not think the act itself particularly important. What was important, in his mind, was whether a Parliament in which the colonies were not represented had the right to impose any internal taxes in America. He did not question the right of London to set custom duties on goods coming into the colonies, but he and many other Americans were sensitive about the difference between such external taxes and those imposed on transactions *within* the colonies. Throughout his stay in England he fought to get this principle accepted. He considered the Stamp Act only a skirmish in the broader battle.

This was one of the few times in his life that Franklin misjudged the temper of his countrymen, for back home the Stamp Act had become a flaming issue. It was attacked as an intolerable violation of colonial rights. There were riots from Massachusetts to Georgia. Stamp tax collectors were tarred and feathered. And Franklin was labeled a villain by many who thought he had not resisted the act forcefully enough. In Philadelphia, his political enemies spread the rumor that he had been bribed to favor the act, and there was angry talk of burning his house. His son William, who was now governor of New Jersey, hastened home to take his mother and sister to safety. Deborah let Sally go, but did not leave herself. She sent for two male relatives, telling them to bring guns. Then she barricaded the house and waited for the mob. It never came.

Franklin was disturbed by the violence back home and undertook to get the Stamp Act repealed. He had the support of many British merchants who were opposed to the act because angry colonists had stopped buying British goods. These businessmen had some influence in the House of Commons, and Franklin persuaded them to get a hearing by

This British cartoon, published two weeks after the repeal of the Stamp Act, shows Prime Minister George Grenville (fourth from left) burying his dead brainchild. The coffin is being carried to a "family vault," where other unwise laws lie interred.

the House to consider the act's repeal. He said that he would be glad to testify. At the hearing, in February, 1766, Franklin answered a barrage of questions—carefully prepared ones from friendly members and difficult ones from hostile members. He built his case on two main points: that England would lose more by enforcing the act than she would gain from the stamp revenues, and that there was great doubt that the act could be administered at all in the face of widespread resistance. Franklin's arguments were so compelling and the merchants so numerous that Parliament voted to repeal the act within the month.

From a villain, Franklin became a hero in America. Toasts were drunk to him throughout the colonies as word of his success spread. But Franklin himself was far from satisfied. The repeal legislation contained a clause that Parliament had the right to make laws for the colonies "in all cases whatsoever." No consideration had been given to his proposal that representatives from the colonies be allowed seats in Parliament. The repeal of the Stamp Act, in sum, did little to establish the principles for which Franklin was fighting.

For the next nine years, Franklin continued his battle for colonial rights and representation, striving to gain for Americans the privileges of Englishmen. He did not want a revolution that would sever the colonies from the mother country. But neither did he want his land ruled simply for England's economic benefit. American colonists had been selling raw materials to England at low cost, and had been forced to buy back high-priced goods which they were not allowed to manufacture in the colonies.

Franklin believed that reasonable men could bring about an acceptable and peaceful trade relationship between the two lands. Even in the early 1770's, as colonial attitudes toward England became more and more explosive, Franklin counseled moderation. "As between friends every affront is not worth a duel," he wrote, "between nations every injury is not worth a war."

This was a difficult period in Franklin's life. He was a philosopher of the age of reason, but he was caught between two forces of unreason. To King George III and his stubborn ministers, talk of colonial rights was like a red cloth to a bull. On the other side of the ocean, a growing number of men were calling revolution the only means of obtaining their rights—men such as Samuel Adams, Patrick Henry, and the militant members of the anti-British Sons of Liberty.

Instead of armed violence, Franklin urged the colonies to unite in a total boycott of English goods. He was certain that the boycott would put economic pressure on British laborers and businessmen, and that they in turn would force a change in London's attitude. Meanwhile, Franklin tried to rally English public opinion

around the minority that sympathized with colonial grievances. Among the devices to which he resorted were his "hoaxes."

The most famous of these was "The Edict of the King of Prussia," an announcement in several English newspapers in the name of King Frederick of Prussia. Because England had originally been settled by colonists from Germany, the notice said, Frederick still had the right to make laws governing the country. There followed a list of things that Frederick ordered "his colonists in England" to do. For instance, they were to send their iron ore to Prussia to be smelted and their beaver skins to be made into hats—although he would graciously allow the English to buy back the hats. All of the requirements listed were the same that England had imposed on her American colonies.

Most intelligent British readers knew that this was a clever way of pointing out the unfairness of the English regulations, and many suspected that Franklin had written the "Edict." But there were some gullible people who gazed fearfully across the Channel, waiting for Frederick to appear with an army to enforce his orders. In late 1773—despite his efforts to persuade the English to adopt a more reasonable policy—Franklin was pessimistic about the prospects for a peaceful settlement of colonial problems. Early the next year, when word of the Boston Tea Party reached London, Franklin gave up nearly all

News of the Boston Tea Party, shown above, reached London just as Franklin was to appear before the Privy Council's hearing on the Massachusetts governor. Many members of the council took out their bitterness regarding the incident on Franklin, although he disapproved of the dumping of the tea.

hope. He called the dumping of tea into Boston harbor "an act of violent injustice" and offered to pay for the ruined tea himself—if England would repeal the tea tax. But his voice of moderation at this time was drowned out by the shouts of denunciation against Franklin himself. The immediate occasion for the clamor against the American might be called The Case of the Hutchinson Letters.

Thomas Hutchinson, the American-born governor of Massachusetts, had written some letters to a member of the British Ministry, suggesting that strong measures be used in dealing with the colonies. Somehow the letters had been given to Franklin—with the stipulation that he should neither copy nor print them, and that he must never disclose the name of the man who gave them to him.

Franklin, in turn, sent the letters to the Massachusetts Committee of Correspondence, insisting that they be kept secret. Samuel Adams read the letters to a secret session of the Assembly; but inevitably, the information leaked out and was pounced upon by the colonial newspapers.

The publication of these private letters brought about a scandal in London. A man named William Whately claimed that they had been addressed to his brother, who had since died, and that a friend of Franklin's named John Temple had stolen them. Whately and Temple fought a duel in which Whately was wounded. Then Franklin, in order to

prevent further bloodshed, published an announcement saying, "I alone am the person who obtained and transmitted to Boston the letters in question." Meanwhile, the Massachusetts Assembly petitioned for the removal of Governor Hutchinson, the author of the letters.

By this time the king's ministers were very anxious to get rid of Franklin. They believed, or pretended to believe, that he was behind all the unrest in the colonies. To keep him quiet, they tried to bribe him with a well-paying post in the English government. When this did not work, they decided to use the king's Privy Council hearing on the Massachusetts petition against Hutchinson to ruin Franklin's reputation.

It was at this hearing that Wedderburn, chosen for his vindictive tongue, attacked Franklin while supposedly defending Hutchinson. Franklin, as an expression of contempt for the true purpose of the hearing, refused to respond to the scathing insults Wedderburn hurled at him. Nothing he could have said would have affected the obviously hostile committee. The petition for the removal of Governor Hutchinson was turned down without discussion, and the day after the

Letters from the American-born governor of Massachusetts, Thomas Hutchinson (right), were the first step in a chain of events that led to Franklin's denouncement in London. In the letters, the governor suggested the use of force to put down colonial disturbances.

hearing, Franklin was removed from his post as deputy postmaster general, which he had continued to hold while in England. Friends reported that there was some talk of sending Franklin to prison, and that Franklin had thought of burning his papers. In any event, whatever influence he had had in official circles was apparently gone.

Although his prestige in London was at a low ebb, Franklin's popularity in the colonies was still rising. Shortly after the Hutchinson hearing, he received a message from the First Continental Congress—a meeting of twelve colonies to protest disciplinary action imposed by Parliament after the Boston Tea Party. The Congress was sending a formal petition to the king, and although Franklin had thought of going home, he now felt that he must remain to help his countrymen present it.

While he waited for the petition to arrive, Deborah died in Philadelphia. It had been nine years since he had last seen her there; he had several times tried to persuade her to come to London, but she had an unreasoned terror of an ocean voyage, and refused to make the trip. Perhaps her decision had been the right one. Although Deborah had been the loyal and capable wife of a Philadelphia tradesman, she would have been uncomfortable in the sophisticated European circles in which her husband moved.

At the same time, Franklin became involved unwittingly in another intrigue. It started when two influential English Quakers called on Franklin to tell him that some of the king's ministers would like to effect a peaceful settlement with the colonies. If Franklin would compile a list of conditions under which this could be accomplished, they would see that it got to the right people. Although Franklin protested that nothing he did now would be given serious consideration, the Quakers assured him that his name would be kept out of it. Franklin then drew up a list of seventeen points—the same issues he had always thought necessary to avert a break between England and the colonies. He offered no compromise.

The next act in this drama was played, along with a game of chess, in the drawing room of Lady Howe— sister of Lord Richard Howe, rear admiral and member of Parliament. A fellow member of the Royal Society had approached Franklin at a meeting and said that her ladyship would like to play chess with him, fancying she could win. Franklin agreed and had a delightful game—although the winner is unknown. During a second game, Lady Howe told Franklin that several of the ministers were ashamed of the way he had been treated, adding, "I wish the government would employ you to settle the dispute for them. I am sure that nobody could do it so well."

At another game the purpose of the chess playing was disclosed: actually, the games had been planned by Lord

Franklin played several games of chess with Lord Richard Howe's sister (above). Franklin did not realize initially that she was playing another game at the same time, involving her influential brother and very high stakes.

*Franklin drew this gruesome cartoon and distributed engravings
of it as tensions mounted between England and the colonies. It
shows Great Britain dismembered of her four limbs—New York,
New England, Pennsylvania, and Virginia. The British ships in
the background have brooms tied to the tops of their masts, in-
dicating they are for sale due to the loss of colonial trade.*

REDUC'D

Howe so that he could talk informally with Franklin about colonial affairs. His Lordship told Franklin that he had seen his seventeen points and that they were unacceptable as they stood. If concessions were made, Howe said, Franklin might "with reason expect any reward in the power of the government to bestow."

Lord Howe and the ministers for whom he and the two Quakers were acting were convinced that Franklin's influence in the colonies was so great that the Americans would accept any proposals he favored. It seemed to them—unaccustomed to honest government—merely a case of setting the bribe high enough. They obviously did not know their man. Pressed by Lord Howe, Franklin submitted a new list, but it amounted to a re-wording of his seventeen points. At this impasse, Lord Howe withdrew as England's peacemaker.

Finally, the petition from the Continental Congress arrived. But it was not even discussed in Parliament. There was no further hope of avoiding a break between the mother country and the colonies. Franklin sailed home across the Atlantic, taking samples of sea water as he went, in an attempt to chart the path of the Gulf Stream. While he was in mid-ocean, on April 19, 1775, American militia at Concord and Lexington exchanged fire with British troops. More than a hundred men died, and the violent rebellion that Franklin had so long worked to avert had begun.

6

"We hold these truths . . ."

When Franklin returned to Philadelphia on May 5, 1775, he was sixty-nine years old. He had suffered several lengthy illnesses while in London, and was subject to increasingly severe attacks of gout. He might well have retired to his scientific pursuits and let younger men carry on the fight. But he now realized sadly that revolution was inevitable, and applied his genius to the American cause with extraordinary vigor.

The day after he reached home, and four days before Ethan Allen captured Fort Ticonderoga from the British, Franklin took a seat in the Second

The members of the drafting committee submit the Declaration of Independence to Congress, June 28, 1776. Shown here are: John Adams (left), Roger Sherman, Robert Livingston, Thomas Jefferson, and Franklin.

Continental Congress as one of the delegates from Pennsylvania. Although Franklin was its oldest member, the Congress made him one of its busiest. They named him postmaster general, to run an American postal service in place of the crown's system. He was also a member of various congressional committees and designed the Continental paper money and supervised its printing. He helped promote the manufacture of saltpeter, an essential ingredient of gunpowder. With Thomas Jefferson of Virginia and John Adams of Massachusetts, he devised a seal for the United States, which was so extravagant that only the motto, *E Pluribus Unum*, and the Eye of Providence were retained. The aging statesman also traveled—to Cambridge, Massachusetts, to confer with General Washington on the or-

Franklin, Jefferson, and Adams produced an unorthodox design for a seal of the United States. One side showed Moses causing the Red Sea to overwhelm his pursuers (top): the reverse side depicted the goddesses of Liberty and Justice, the symbols of six European nations, and the initials of each colony. Here, DC stands for Delaware Colony.

ganization of the army, and to Montreal—an arduous and fruitless journey—to win support for the American revolution from the French Canadians.

When in Philadelphia, Franklin spoke rarely in Congress, which met in the Pennsylvania State House. He had a low opinion of oratory. Through Poor Richard he had said, "Here comes the orator, with his flood of words and his drop of wisdom." And again, "The worst wheel on the cart makes the most noise." Thomas Jefferson, who had great respect for Franklin, wrote: "I served with General Washington in the legislature of Virginia . . . and . . . with Dr. Franklin in Congress. I never heard either of them speak for ten minutes at a time . . . They laid their shoulders to the great points, knowing that the little ones would follow of themselves." John Adams saw it differently. He wrote that in Congress Franklin was seen "from day to day, sitting in silence, a great part of the time fast asleep in his chair."

Adams was annoyed and puzzled by Franklin. The fiery young lawyer, totally involved in the affairs of government, was constantly on his feet, debating, discussing, and proposing measures. Yet, when the speechmaking was over, it was Franklin who was appointed to the important committees. Adams once wrote sarcastically that history would probably tell the story of the Revolution by saying, "Franklin's electrical rod smote the earth and out sprang General Washington . . . Franklin electrified him with his rod—and thenceforward these two conducted all the policy, negotiations, legislatures and war."

While a member of the Continental Congress, Franklin was also a member of the Pennsylvania Assembly and the Committee of Safety. He supervised the building of log and iron obstructions in the Delaware River—which would later prevent his "friend" Lord Howe from sailing upriver to Philadelphia. Franklin designed a pike to be used instead of bayonets, which the Americans lacked, and proposed to counter the shortage of firearms by returning to bows and arrows. "These," he wrote, "were good weapons, not wisely laid aside. . . ."

In this period, Franklin suffered what must have been one of his greatest personal disappointments. He met with his son to induce him to resign from his post as governor of New Jersey, but William, who was a confirmed Tory, refused. Father and son were on opposite sides throughout the war, and never would they be fully reconciled.

In July, 1775—further developing his old Albany Congress plan—Franklin drafted and presented to Congress his *Articles of Confederation and Perpetual Union*, the first concrete plan for the bringing together of what he called "The United Colonies of North America." The articles provided for "common defense against enemies . . . security of liberty and properties . . .

Carpenter's Hall, which held Franklin's subscription library before the war, also housed the First Continental Congress during its momentous sessions in Philadelphia in 1774.

safety of persons and families . . . mutual and general welfare." An elected Congress was to have power to legislate "on peace and war, the entering into alliances and sending ambassadors, the settling of disputes between colony and colony."

The plan did not specifically propose independence, but this was implicit—colonies do not make alliances and send ambassadors. Jefferson and a few others favored the proposal, but Congress took no action on it. The representatives were too jealous of the rights of their own colonies, and too uncertain of the ultimate aims of their rebellion to back Franklin's idea. So the struggling young country fought on, with no true unity.

113

Labeled by his father "a thorough government man," William Franklin had aligned himself with the crown as early as 1765, the year of the Stamp Act crisis. Not long before the Declaration of Independence, he was formally indicted as "an enemy to the liberties of this country," and then imprisoned.

Franklin's most direct contribution to the revolution was to be made through the Congressional Committee of Correspondence. This was America's first state department, empowered to appoint and instruct agents to deal with foreign governments. Franklin was an obvious choice for the committee. He knew hundreds of influential Europeans—scientists, artists, musicians, politicians, publishers, even a few royal rulers. And he was practically the only revolutionary leader widely known across the Atlantic.

When a French agent arrived in Philadelphia in late 1775, it was Franklin who first met with him, and who then led the secret nighttime discussions between the agent and the committee. Franklin told the agent to report to the French foreign minister, the Comte de Vergennes, that Congress would assuredly declare for independence. This was in December, 1775, six months before such a declaration, and Congress had not even considered the issue. But Franklin felt that a declaration of independence was essential if the war was to be won. As long as Americans remained merely colonists in rebellion, they could expect no outside aid from Europe.

To enlist the support of the English people, Franklin had to use more subtle means. Secretly, he wrote to friends in London hoping to strengthen public opinion for the American cause. To Edmund Burke, a member of Parliament and an old friend of Franklin's from his London days, he wrote that the British soldiers at the battles of Lexington and Concord "made a most vigorous retreat—twenty miles in three hours— scarce to be paralleled in history; the feeble Americans, who pelted them all the way, could scarcely keep up with them." After Bunker Hill, Franklin wrote to his scientist friend Joseph Priestley: "Britain, at the expense of three millions, has killed one hundred and fifty Yankees . . . which is twenty thousand pounds a head . . . During the same time sixty thousand children have been born in America."

With the new year, 1776, the pace of revolution accelerated. In January, Thomas Paine sent Franklin a copy of his pamphlet *Common Sense*, a stirring call to independence. Late in February, Parliament declared an absolute blockade of American ports. By April, increasing tensions in the South led colonial governments to instruct their representatives in Congress to vote for independence. Then, on June 7, 1776, Richard Henry Lee of Virginia offered Congress his momentous resolution that "these United Colonies are and of right ought to be, free and independent States."

Despite serious reverses in their war effort, the colonists never ceased lampooning their enemies. In this American cartoon, which was titled British Heroism, *redcoats are launching a fierce assault against some amused cows.*

HENRY E. HUNTINGTON LIBRARY AND ART GALLERY

OVERLEAF: *As this painting by Edward Pine and Edward Savage attests, Congress voted approval of the Declaration of Independence with little furor. Franklin sits pensively in the center foreground of the historic assembly.*

HISTORICAL SOCIETY OF PENNSYLVANIA

A Declaration by the Representatives of the UNITED STATES OF AMERICA, in General Congress assembled.

When in the course of human events it becomes necessary for one people to dissolve the political bands which have connected them with another, and to ~~advance from that subordination in which they have hitherto remained~~, & to assume among the powers of the earth the separate and equal ~~and equal and independent~~ station to which the laws of nature & of nature's god entitle them, a decent respect to the opinions of mankind requires that they should declare the causes which impel them to the separation.

We hold these truths to be self-evident; ~~sacred & undeniable~~ that all men are created equal ~~& independent~~, that ~~from that equal creation they derive rights~~ they are endowed by their creator with ~~inherent & inalienable~~ rights; that among these ~~which~~ are ~~the preservation of life, & liberty, & the pursuit of happiness;~~ life, & liberty, & the pursuit of happiness; that to secure these rights ~~ends~~, governments are instituted among men, deriving their just powers from the consent of the governed; that whenever any form of government becomes ~~shall~~ destructive of these ends, it is the right of the people to alter or to abolish it, & to institute new government, laying it's foundation on such principles & organising it's powers in such form, as to them shall seem most likely to effect their safety & happiness. prudence indeed will dictate that governments long established should not be ~~changed~~ for light & transient causes: and accordingly all experience hath shewn that mankind are more disposed to suffer while evils are sufferable, than to right themselves by abolishing the forms to which they are accustomed. but when a long train of abuses & usurpations [begun at a distinguished period, &] pursuing invariably the same object, evinces a design to ~~subject~~ reduce them + under absolute Despotism ~~to arbitrary power~~, it is their right, it is their duty, to throw off such ~~government~~ + & to provide new guards for their future security. such has been the patient sufferance of these colonies; & such is now the necessity which constrains them to [expunge] ~~alter~~ their former systems of government. the history of the present king of Great Britain ~~his present majesty~~ is a history of [unremitting] ~~repeated~~ injuries and usurpations, [among which appears no solitary fact ~~to prove which let facts be submitted~~] to contradict the uniform tenor of the rest, [all of which ~~but all have~~ have in direct object the establishment of an absolute tyranny over these states. to prove this, let facts be submitted to a candid world [for the truth of which we pledge a faith yet unsullied by falsehood.]

A page of Jefferson's draft of the Declaration, edited by Adams and Franklin, is shown opposite. The official version was approved and signed in Pennsylvania's State House (above), now called Independence Hall.

The moment Franklin had foreseen was at hand. Though ailing and exhausted, he took on the task of preparing a declaration of independence along with Jefferson, Adams, Roger Sherman of Connecticut, and Robert Livingston of New York. Jefferson wrote the original draft. On a copy which still exists, there are several changes in Franklin's handwriting. Most of them are minor, but one has proved enduring and memorable.

Where Jefferson wrote, "We hold these truths to be sacred and undeniable," Franklin crossed out the last three words and added simply, "self-evident."

Jefferson is supposed to have said that the declaration committee would have selected its oldest member and most famous writer to draft the Declaration except that they could not trust him not to put a joke in it. Franklin, in fact, is credited with

119

the only humor associated with the solemn document. As Congress cut and revised Jefferson's carefully worded draft, Franklin leaned over and told him a yarn about a man who was about to go into business as a hatter. He designed a sign that said, over a picture of a hat, "John Thompson, hatter, makes and sells hats for ready money." When he asked several friends for their opinions, each took out a different word. "Hatter" was not necessary with a picture of a hat, one said. "Makes" was superfluous; nobody cared who made them. "Sells" should come out; nobody expected him to give them away. Finally, there was nothing left but "John Thompson" with a picture of a hat.

Another Franklin anecdote connected with the Declaration has become an American legend. Supposedly, as John Hancock signed the document he said, "We must be unanimous; there must be no pulling in different ways; we must all hang together." "Yes," Franklin allegedly added, "we must indeed all hang together or most assuredly we shall all hang separately."

Within a week after the Declaration of Independence was announced, Lord Howe, commanding a British fleet, joined his brother General Howe in New York and again took up the role of peacemaker. He sent Franklin a friendly letter in which he mentioned the king's desire for peace, and offered pardons to all rebels—except

John Adams, who had been particularly annoying to George III. Franklin answered the amicable letter with a grim one, pointing out to Howe that the colonists were the injured parties and saying that England's "atrocious injuries have extinguished every remaining spark of affection for that parent country we once held dear."

But Lord Howe persevered, and paroled a captured American general, John Sullivan, to carry a message to Congress. In it, Howe requested that representatives meet him on Staten Island. Franklin, Adams, and Edward Rutledge of South Carolina went to the meeting, but nothing came of it, for the antagonists were too far apart.

In the last half of 1776, the British stepped up their campaign and the American troops barely survived one battle only to find themselves engaged in another. That August, Washington was defeated on Long Island, narrowly escaping complete disaster by fleeing with his army to Manhattan Island. As part of the British plan to cut New England off from the rest of the colonies, Britain's General Guy Carleton was marching down from Canada to join forces with General Howe in New York. The American cause had never been so hopeless. Again the Congress turned to Franklin, its most experienced diplomat, sending him to Paris to enlist France's aid, which was desperately needed.

If encouraged by the proceedings in Philadelphia, the colonists' spirit was soon dampened by Washington's defeat on Long Island. Above, rear-guard American units finally retreat across Long Island's Gowanus Creek.

7

War by Diplomacy

During the first days of December, 1776, the American armed sloop *Reprisal* sailed swiftly but cautiously toward France. The waters near Europe were patrolled by swifter, more heavily armed English ships, which the *Reprisal* sought to avoid with particular care. For she carried a distinguished passenger who undoubtedly would be hanged for treason if captured.

The prospect of capture did not seem to bother the passenger, however. He was a kind-looking old man who calmly went about taking temperatures of the air and water—continuing the studies of the Gulf Stream that he had begun in more peaceful days. Helping him were two boys, aged seven and sixteen, his grandsons.

When Benjamin Franklin stepped ashore in France, he was wearing his customary plain clothing and a fur hat to protect his head against the cold of the wintry Atlantic. His appearance immediately delighted the French. He looked like old Father Abraham in *The Way to Wealth*. Moreover, he fit the Frenchman's romantic idea of an American—a kind and simple person full of backwoods virtues.

The old man was not from the back woods and he was far from simple; but if the French chose to think of him as such, the impression, he realized, might be helpful in his delicate and vitally important dealings with

When Franklin was in Paris trying to form an alliance with France, he often wore a fur hat which made him look like a frontiersman. Based on a contemporary French engraving, this portrait is probably by John Trumbull.

123

them. So he continued to support the impression, even in Paris. Throughout his stay in France, Franklin moved among the brilliant silks and powdered wigs of French society with his plain clothes and straight gray hair, often wearing his fur cap, always enjoying his special prominence—like a gray gull in a cage full of colorful parrots.

Franklin was one of three commissioners—easily the foremost in reputation—selected by the Continental Congress to seek aid from France. If possible, they were to negotiate an out-and-out military alliance. One commissioner, Silas Deane of Connecticut, was already in France. He had arrived in July to handle a secret arrangement under which France was permitting some arms to trickle out to Haiti and Martinique in the Caribbean, there to be picked up by American ships. Arthur Lee of Virginia came over from London—where he had been a colonial agent—as the third commissioner.

As the unofficial chief of the American mission, Franklin started his diplomatic maneuvering on several fronts. To men in the government he talked about how England, France's traditional enemy, would be all-powerful if the colonies were defeated. To the businessmen he talked about how valuable trade with America would be if it were no longer a British monopoly. To the people generally he talked about liberty and freedom.

During his first year in Paris, however, Franklin and his fellow commissioners made little tangible progress. Swaying the young French king, Louis XVI, to the cause of republican America was not an easy job. Louis had no love for George III of England, but they were fellow monarchs, and it disturbed him to support any subjects in rebellion against their king. Louis' foreign minister, the Comte de Vergennes, favored the cause of the colonies because he felt that American success would weaken England, but he was cautious. He knew that if Britain defeated the colonies, she would quickly turn on anyone in Europe who had helped them. And that first year the war was continuing to go against the colonies. News of the British success at Fort Ticonderoga and of the capture of Philadelphia did not help Franklin's cause in France.

Then, on the morning of December 4, 1777, word arrived of Burgoyne's defeat at Saratoga. Franklin rushed the news to Vergennes, along with a new draft of a proposed treaty of alliance. Vergennes took the draft to the king; and at a secret night meeting several days later, he told Franklin that Louis was willing to sign—but only if Spain signed at the same time. Spain, however, was even more reluctant than France to commit herself to the American cause. She feared that a successful revolution in North America would create unrest in her colonies in Central and South America.

While negotiations with France

and Spain continued, Britain's chief intelligence agent, Paul Wentworth, arrived secretly in Paris in mid-December. He was sent to feel out the commissioners on prospects for a truce and negotiations for peace. Franklin refused to see Wentworth, but Silas Deane had several meetings with him and Franklin made sure that Vergennes heard about the meetings. Only when King Louis proposed to delay signing the treaty—in view of Spain's hesitation—did Franklin himself send for Wentworth.

The British spy reported the meeting fully to his superiors. He was very confused by the way Franklin acted: "Nobody says less, generally, and keeps a point more closely in view, but he was diffuse and unmethodical today." Apparently it never occurred to Wentworth that Franklin was merely using him.

The meeting had its desired effect. A rumor swept through Paris that Britain and the colonies were about to make peace and that the Americans would then join the British in conquering the French and Spanish colonies in the West Indies. Louis promptly agreed to the treaty without waiting for Spain. (Later, however, Spain did join the fight against England, as did Holland.)

The Comte de Vergennes (top), France's foreign minister and an extremely capable statesman, sought revenge against England for the losses she had inflicted on his country in European wars. Of Franklin's associates, Silas Deane (center) was the best diplomat, but eventually his reputation was ruined by the third commissioner, Arthur Lee (bottom).

Though youthful and haughty, Louis XVI (left) was clever enough to see the advantages of an American alliance, which according to some sources was made on the king's decision alone. Six weeks after the treaty of alliance was signed, Louis formally received Franklin, Deane, and Lee at Versailles (below).

When Franklin arrived at the ministry of foreign affairs on February 6, 1778, to sign the treaty, he had on the same old velvet coat that he had worn the day before. The treaty was supposed to have been signed then but was put off because of the French minister's cold. Silas Deane noticed Franklin wearing the coat two days in a row and asked him why. "To give it a little revenge," Franklin answered. "I wore this coat on the day Wedderburn abused me at Whitehall."

The matter of alliance was settled by the treaty, which has been called a diplomatic victory comparable to the military one at Saratoga. But the matter of aid, French aid in particular, remained urgent. Although French troops and the French fleet were of great help to the colonies, especially in the final battles, what the Americans needed most immediately from France was money to maintain their own army. Throughout the war, it was Franklin's main job to secure this money in loans and gifts from the French, a job made no easier by the unwise fiscal policies of the Continental Congress.

From Philadelphia, Franklin would receive authorization to apply for loans—not when he thought the best moment for asking arose, but when Congress decided it needed more money. Then Congress would spend the money, on credit, before Franklin had even raised it. He always managed to get continued French assistance, but he said he spent many sleepless nights worrying about it.

Although Vergennes favored all-out aid to the colonies, other ministers did not. Turgot, the minister of finance, begrudged every franc that left his treasury. Franklin had to use all his charms to gain approval of the loans, and for this his personal popularity with the French was worth millions to the colonies.

His fame had grown steadily since his arrival. France was flooded with miniature paintings of the quiet New World philosopher, set in rings and on the lids of snuffboxes. His picture was proudly hung over fireplaces throughout the country. In a letter to his daughter, Sally, he wrote, "These . . . pictures, busts and prints . . . have made your father's face as well known as that of the moon, so that he durst not do anything which would oblige him to run away, as his phiz [slang for physiognomy, or face] would discover him wherever he should venture to show it."

Even John Adams, who continued to dislike Franklin, was impressed by his great popularity in France. "Franklin's reputation," Adams wrote, "was more universal than that of Leibnitz or Newton, Frederick or

OVERLEAF: *Carrying a tricorn instead of his fur cap, but otherwise dressed in typically simple clothes, Franklin receives a crown of laurel in an elegant chamber of Versailles. Looking on with admiring gazes are many notables of the French court, as well as the king and Marie Antoinette (seated at right).*
COLLECTION OF GRAEME LORIMER

127

Voltaire, and his character more beloved and esteemed than any or all of them . . . His name was familiar to government and people, to kings, courtiers, nobility, clergy and philosophers, as well as to plebians, to such a degree that there was scarcely a peasant or a citizen, a *valet de chambre*, coachman or footman, a lady's chambermaid or a scullion in a kitchen who was not familiar with it and who did not consider him a friend to humankind . . . When they spoke of him they seemed to think that he would restore the golden age."

Adams had arrived in France in April, 1778, to replace Deane, who had been recalled by the Congress because of critical reports concerning him sent by Arthur Lee, the third commissioner. Lee, suspicious of everyone, thought Deane was gaining personally from transactions between France and the Congress. Adams soon decided that the American mission would operate more efficiently with one commissioner than with three. Both he and Franklin wrote members of Congress to this effect, and in September the Congress revoked the three commissions and named Franklin the sole minister to the French court.

He was given the resounding title of Minister Plenipotentiary, but his duties were not always so exalted. Among the tasks that irritated Franklin was the screening of foreign officers who wanted to serve in the Continental Army. Nearly every European who desired a commission in the army came to Franklin for a recommendation. Some he could not avoid for political reasons—if, for instance, the applicant was proposed by Vergennes. Franklin wrote to Washington apologizing for the men that he felt obliged to send. But in one case he sensed that a needy German captain, Baron Friedrich von Steuben, would be a welcome addition to Washington's army, and in his letter of recommendation he said the baron had been "lately a lieutenant-general in the king of Prussia's service." The high rank that Franklin conferred upon the captain so impressed Congress that it sent von Steuben to Washington at Valley Forge, and thereby provided a crack drillmaster who soon turned the ragged militia into a disciplined fighting force.

Another foreign officer of Revolutionary fame with whom Franklin was concerned was the Marquis de Lafayette. Friends of Lafayette in France wanted to send the young nobleman a large sum of money to help support him in America, but they knew he was much too liberal a spender and would soon go through it all. They approached Franklin, who then wrote to Washington asking the general to dole out the money in small sums to the marquis and "take occasion to advise him [on spending it], if necessary, with a friendly affection."

Lafayette returned to Paris for a leave in February, 1779. With the enthusiastic young officer at hand,

The Bonhomme Richard *(left) and the* Serapis *pound each other to pieces just off the English coast. Out of the fight came a great victory for John Paul Jones and many diplomatic benefits for Franklin; yet the American ship was so battered that it sank two days later.*

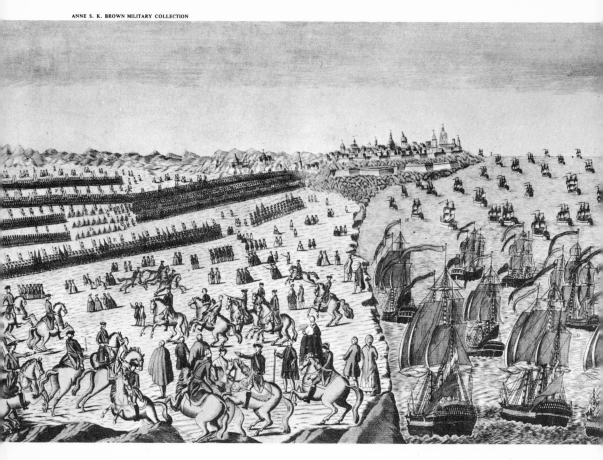

Franklin put aside his diplomatic duties long enough to become involved with him and John Paul Jones in a scheme to invade England. The French marquis would command the landing force; the Scotch-born American, the fleet. Franklin had come to know Jones while helping him to obtain a ship, a French merchant vessel that Jones named the *Bonhomme Richard* after Franklin's Poor Richard.

Toward the daring invasion plan, the old philosopher contributed some sound suggestions as to how Lafayette should employ his cavalry after he landed. King Louis, however, diverted the troops that Lafayette had counted on for the land operation, but

This comically unrealistic view of the British surrender at Yorktown was engraved by a Frenchman, who filled it with French ships, French troops, and French officers on rearing horses. What mattered to the Americans was that the victory insured their independence.

the sea expedition continued according to plan. Jones was skirting the east coast of England when, on September 23, 1779, he won his famous victory over the British ship of war *Serapis*.

In spite of his participation in military affairs, the inhumanities of war greatly distressed Franklin. Writing to his English friend Edmund Burke, he said, "Since the foolish part of mankind will make wars . . . not having sense enough otherwise to

132

settle their differences, it certainly becomes the wiser part, who cannot prevent these wars, to alleviate as much as possible the calamities attending them." On his own authority Franklin issued safe-conduct passports to British ships carrying supplies to a Moravian colony in Labrador. He also sent orders to the commanders of all ships acting for Congress that they were not to molest the English explorer and geographer, Captain Cook, who was then involved in important scientific research.

American revolutionary forces, meanwhile, were having trouble at home. Militarily, they were steadily losing ground. Financially, the Continental Congress' reckless handling of money led to a monetary crisis in March, 1780. Unpaid soldiers were mutinying, and Washington wrote to Franklin saying that more money was needed or America would have to sue for peace. Early in 1781, King Louis agreed to make a gift of a large amount of money on the condition that only Washington be allowed to spend it. Congress was annoyed—spending money was its prerogative. But Franklin wrote simply that he could not argue with the king, because the money was a gift, not a loan, and every donor had "the right of qualifying his gifts with such terms as he thinks proper." Since Louis was more interested in tinkering with locks and hunting boar than in the details of finance, it is not unlikely that the idea of placing the money in

Washington's hands originated with Franklin—who knew that the general would use it to the best advantage.

America's fortunes shifted decisively in 1781. For most Americans, the Revolutionary War ended on October 19, 1781, when Cornwallis surrendered at Yorktown. But for Franklin, it continued for two more years while he endeavored to negotiate a peace. "'Blessed are the peacemakers' is, I suppose, to be understood in the other world," Franklin wrote to Adams soon after both men were named peace commissioners, "for in this [world] they are frequently cursed. Being as yet rather too much attached to this world, I have therefore not ambition to be concerned in fabricating this peace . . . I esteem it, however, as an honour."

The honor was conferred on John Jay of New York, Henry Laurens of South Carolina, and Thomas Jefferson, as well as on Franklin and Adams. This array of strong personalities who made up the American peace commission was bound to be in conflict. But as the first overtures of peace were heard, Franklin, for a while, was able to handle matters by himself. Adams was in Holland negotiating a loan; Jay, the minister to Spain, was in Madrid; Laurens, captured at sea in 1780, was a prisoner in the Tower of London; and Jefferson, busy with internal affairs at home, never did serve. All were elsewhere when on March 22, 1782, Franklin in France was informed that Lord Shelburne, an influ-

133

ential Englishman friendly to the American cause, would be pleased to hear from him.

Franklin did not know that two days before, Lord Shelburne had been named secretary of state for colonial affairs in a government upheaval that had brought more pro-American men to power. He immediately replied, however, telling Shelburne that he was sure his lordship, "with all good men," desired a general peace, "which I wish to see before I die; and to which I shall, with infinite pleasure, contribute everything in my power."

Shelburne responded by sending Richard Oswald, a British diplomat, to call on Franklin. Oswald told Franklin that the new ministry would agree to American independence and would make peace with France and America jointly. He asked Franklin on what terms the colonies would agree to peace.

Franklin suggested that the British voluntarily give up Canada. "Perhaps America will not demand it," he said, "but on the mind of the people in general would it not have an excellent effect if Britain should voluntarily offer to give up this province?" He went on to point out that England derived little good from Canada except the fur trade, while the gesture of renouncing Canada would go a long

This painting of the Paris peace conference by Benjamin West was never finished. The English commissioners refused to be in the picture, and the Americans' portraits were painted from existing art works. They are (from left): John Jay, John Adams, Franklin, Henry Laurens, and Franklin's grandson and secretary William Temple Franklin.

The eighteenth century was an age when artists mixed allegory with art, and Franklin was no exception, having helped design the medal at left to commemorate American independence. As a famous person, he appeared in many allegories himself. The one below shows him in classic drapery, directing an attack on Tyranny and Avarice from the clouds.

way toward making Americans feel less bitter about the homes and property destroyed by British troops.

Later, Franklin gave Oswald eight specific points—four that he knew the colonies would demand and four that he considered desirable. The first four were: recognition of independence; a settlement of western boundaries; a restriction of the boundary of Canada; and "freedom of fishing on the Bank of Newfoundland, as well for fish as whales." The four desirable points were: compensation for property that had been destroyed; some kind of expression from Parliament that it had been in the wrong; reciprocal shipping and trading rights; and "giving up every part of Canada."

In late June, 1782, while Franklin was meeting with Oswald, John Jay arrived in Paris and soon objected to dealing with Oswald because the Englishman's commission as a negotiator was not worded to Jay's satisfaction. It authorized Oswald to deal with the commissioners of "said colonies and plantations." Jay insisted that the wording must be changed to authorize Oswald to deal with the United States of America. Jay felt that the terms of the treaty would be more favorable to the Americans if the two countries negotiated as equals. He wanted England to acknowledge America's independence first and then make a treaty —not to make independence part of the treaty.

Franklin saw no point to this legalistic dispute. The important thing in his mind was independence, not how Oswald's commission was worded. But when Adams arrived in Paris in October, he sided with Jay, and from that point on Franklin was generally overruled. His only further contribution to the negotiations came at the end, when the British negotiators seemed reluctant to sign the treaty they had all but agreed upon. Franklin told the British that if there was to be a further delay the Americans might well increase their demands. The British signed a provisional treaty on November 30—a treaty that was almost identical with Franklin's first four points.

Immediately after the signing, Franklin wrote to Congress, saying: "I am now entering my seventy-eighth year; public business has engrossed fifty of them; I wish now to be, for the little time I have left, my own master. If I live to see this peace concluded, I shall beg leave to remind Congress of their promise then to dismiss me. I shall be happy to sing with Old Simeon: 'Now lettest thy servant depart in peace, for mine eyes have seen salvation.'"

Franklin's final words on the war were penned in a letter to an old friend shortly after the signing of formal treaties between America and France and England on September 3, 1783. "We are now friends with England and with all mankind," he wrote. "May we never see another war! For in my opinion there never was a good war or a bad peace."

Dr Benjamin Franklin, F. R. S.
Sometime Governer of Pennsylvan
Aged 84

8

Franklin's Legacy

Benjamin Franklin had spent nearly thirty years abroad in the service of his country when he asked the Continental Congress to relieve him. Still, it was two years after the signing of the peace treaty before Congress got around to letting its old servant "depart in peace." Thomas Jefferson replaced the beloved minister in 1786—succeeded him, that is. Nobody, said Jefferson, could replace Franklin. Although Jefferson himself was much admired by the French people, he found "more respect and veneration attached to the character of Dr. Franklin in France than to that of

Although its precise date is unknown, this classic silhouette is regarded as the last likeness of the "Sometime Governor of Pennsylvania." It was done by Joseph Sansom, whose initials appear after Franklin's name.

any other person, foreign or native."

The two years after the signing of the treaty and before Jefferson took over from Franklin were relatively leisurely ones for Franklin. Soon after the Revolution, he negotiated a final loan from France and signed America's first postwar commercial treaty, with Sweden. (The king of Sweden insisted that Franklin be the American representative to sign the treaty.) The former postmaster advised the British government on re-establishing postal relations with her former colonies, and he devised a system that both England and France adopted for sending their transatlantic mail packets. But such duties became less time-consuming after an American consul arrived to relieve Franklin of his commercial duties.

Franklin spent these final years

abroad on a small estate in Passy where he had lived during his years in France. In this suburb of Paris, the old sage won the undying affections of the brilliant Madame Helvétius, a widow, and of the entrancing Madame Brillon, the young wife of a French treasury official. During the Revolution, he had turned again to his first love, printing, and had set up a press in his home at Passy. Now he used it to print his "bagatelles"—delightful pieces of humorous writing, which he addressed mainly to these feminine neighbors.

He also wrote and printed more serious material. As soon as the war was over, he was deluged by requests for information from people all over Europe who were thinking of emigrating to America and wanted to know what it was like. So Franklin wrote a paper that he called *Information to Those Who Would Remove to America*. In it he pointed out that there were many mistaken ideas about America. He said that immigrants were welcome if they wanted to work and that there was great opportunity—especially for farmers and artisans. But there were no well-paying government jobs or high posts in the army, and a man's noble birth would not help him in the New World. When people asked about a stranger, Franklin said, it was not "What is he?" but "What can he do?" "In short," Franklin concluded, "America is the land of labor, and by no means what the English call *Lub-*

Before leaving France, Franklin cultivated the friendship of Madame Helvétius (shown above with her family, before her husband's death); and he witnessed the first free ascent of a hot air balloon in 1783 (left).

berland, and the French *Pays de Cocagne* [imaginary lands of idleness and plenty], where the streets are said to be paved with half-peck loaves, the houses tiled with pancakes, and where the fowls fly around ready roasted, crying, *Come eat me."*

In addition to his publications, there was the usual flow of letters from Franklin, many of which eventually found their way into print. They embraced the huge variety of subjects that interested Franklin. He considered a proposed organization in America that would bestow lordly titles and privileges upon members and their descendants—he thought

141

The work of unifying the colonies, begun at the Albany Congress, is finished at last. In this twentieth-century

ainting, Franklin (far left) watches George Washington accept the signed Constitution on September 17, 1787.

In this scene designed for a French bedspread, Franklin and the Spirit of Liberty are being led toward the Temple of Fame by Columbia. The scene has been copied for fabrics in a guest room of the White House.

it was foolish. He objected to the bald eagle as a symbol for America— he called the bird "a rank coward" and proposed the turkey instead. He examined dueling, the death sentence, and the production of luxuries—and condemned them all.

During this period when there were fewer official demands on his time, Franklin hoped to return to his scientific experiments. He did not get around to doing so, but he did keep in touch with European scientists and their work. He was particularly interested in the novel activity of ballooning. Several daring Frenchmen were going aloft at this time in baskets hung beneath giant cloth bags filled with hot air or hydrogen. Other than envisioning a kind of airborne warfare, Franklin had little idea of what

air travel would prove, no more than he had foreseen the eventual applications of his own discoveries in electricity. But he was open-minded as always. When an observer at a balloon ascension in Paris remarked to Franklin, "But what good is it?" the old philosopher replied, *"Eh, a quoi bon l'enfant qui vient de naître?"* (Of what good is a newborn baby?)

Franklin later imagined one purely fanciful purpose for balloons: an airborne carriage pulled about by a man on the ground. Such a carriage, Franklin mused, might make travel tolerable for him. As it was, a kidney stone was already limiting Franklin's physical activity; it made the jarring voyages on the rough roads of that day an anguishing prospect. When, on May 2, 1785, Franklin received word from Congress that he could at last come home, he was not sure he could survive the trip. But adventuresome as ever, he set out—after ten weeks of official and personal farewells. From Passy, he traveled to Le Havre in a litter, loaned by Queen Marie Antoinette. Among the many parting gifts in his baggage was a present from the French government of a small portrait of King Louis set with 408 diamonds. Among his memories must have been the poignant parting scene described by his grandson Benjamin Bache—"of a very great concourse of the people of Passy; a mournful silence reigned around him, and was only interrupted by a few sobs."

Franklin himself had his regrets about leaving, in spite of his desire to see his homeland again. "I am here among a people that love and respect me," he wrote his son William before his departure, "and perhaps I may conclude to die among them; for my friends in America are dying off one after another, and I have been so long abroad that I should now be almost a stranger in my own country."

At the end of a placid sea voyage, however, he found himself greeted not as a stranger but as an extraordinarily popular hero. Franklin landed in Philadelphia amid the booms of cannon salutes and the clangs of pealing church bells. His welcome was a week-long affair in which he received a continual parade of leading citizens. Almost immediately Franklin was nominated by both of Pennsylvania's major parties for a seat on the state's Supreme Executive Council. A month later, easily elected, he was named president of the council. When the General Assembly met, he was named the chief executive of the state.

The job apparently was as much honorary as administrative under Franklin, for it left him time to look after long-neglected personal affairs, including the enlargement of his home on Market Street. He was also able to design some ingenious, if minor, devices in this period: a fan that worked with the touch of the foot so that he could cool himself while reading; a chair that opened into a stepladder like a present-day kitchen stool; and a mechanical hand to take books from high shelves.

Franklin hoped to be able to devote himself at last, now that he was over eighty, to the scientific researches that he had so often put aside for public service. But his energies, though rapidly waning, were once again needed for a public cause. In March, 1787, he was named a Pennsylvania delegate to a convention, soon to meet in Philadelphia, which would seek to draft a constitution for the newly formed United States.

Like George Washington, who was president of the Constitutional Convention, Franklin contented himself mainly with advising the younger members of the convention, and leading them to compromise when they came in conflict with each other.

Some of Franklin's ideas were turned down. For instance, he favored an executive branch of the government consisting of three men, like Roman consuls, instead of a single president. He was opposed to paying salaries to high government officers; he felt that paying lawmakers high salaries might attract the wrong type of man. And he advocated, at first, a legislature consisting of a single body instead of two houses.

It was in the formation of the legislature, however, that Franklin made his greatest contribution to the Constitution. A major stumbling block had been the question of representation in the legislative branch. Massachusetts, Virginia, and Pennsylvania had almost 40 per cent of the country's prospective voters. They wanted representation based on population. The ten less populous states wanted to have an equal number of representatives from each state. Franklin asked both sides to give in a little, saying, "When a broad table is to be made, and the edges of the planks do not fit, the artist takes a little from both and makes a good joint. In like manner here both sides must part with some of their demands."

Franklin soon afterward proposed the plan that was finally accepted: (1) a House of Representatives which would have one member from each state for every 40,000 inhabitants (later amended to 30,000); (2) a Senate in which each state would have an equal number of votes; (3) all money bills would originate in the House and not be subject to revision in the Senate. Without this compromise, there is good chance that the convention's delegates might have dispersed without coming to any agreement.

For the duration of the convention, Franklin remained largely in the background until it came time to sign. On the last day, September 17, 1787, he rose painfully to announce his speech, which another member read for him and which has been judged one of the most eloquent expressions of the whole convention. In it Franklin said: "I confess that there are several parts of this Constitution which I do not at present approve, but I am not sure I shall never approve them; for, having lived long, I have experienced many instances of being obliged by better information or fuller consideration to change opinions, even on important subjects, which I once thought right but found to be otherwise. It is therefore that the older I grow the more apt I am to doubt my own judgment and to pay attention to the judgment of others . . . Though many private persons think . . . highly of their infallibility . . . few express it so naturally as a certain French lady who in dispute

Even before his life's work was completed, Franklin was widely regarded as the greatest, most virtuous man of his age. The French engraver of this ornate tribute set a portrait of Franklin into a frame held by Diogenes —the Greek philosopher who is thought to have searched the world for an honest man.

STUPETE GENTES REPERIT VIVUM DIOGENES

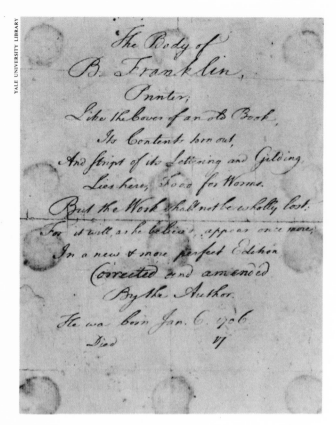

The Body of
B. Franklin,
Printer;
Like the Cover of an old Book,
Its Contents torn out,
And stript of its Lettering and Gilding,
Lies here, Food for Worms.
But the Work shall not be wholly lost:
For it will, as he believ'd, appear once more,
In a new & more perfect Edition
Corrected and amended
By the Author.
He was born Jan. 6. 1706.
Died   17

"B. J. Franklin is dead." Thus, in stark, simple terms the print at right announced to France the death of a patriot who was described by a French statesman, as "one of the greatest men who have ever been engaged in the service of philosophy and of liberty." At left is the famous epitaph written impetuously by Franklin some sixty-two years before his death. His gravestone, however, was inscribed, as his will directed, "Benjamin and Deborah Franklin, 1790."

with her sister said: 'I don't know how it happens, sister, but I meet with nobody but myself that's always in the right.'

"In these sentiments, Sir, I agree to this Constitution with all its faults, if they are such . . . I doubt . . . whether any other convention we can obtain may be able to make a better Constitution . . . The opinions I have had of its errors I sacrifice to the public good. I have never whispered a syllable of them abroad. Within these walls they were born, and here they shall die. . . ."

While the last members of the convention signed the historic document,

Franklin, according to James Madison, looked toward George Washington's chair where a tapestry decorated with the sun was hanging and said, " 'I have often . . . in the course of the session . . . looked behind the president without being able to tell whether [the sun] was rising or setting. But now at length I have the happiness to know that it is a rising and not a setting sun.' "

When Franklin signed the Constitution, he became the only one of the Founding Fathers to endorse all four of the major documents that made possible America's independence and nationality—the others

B.J. FRANKLIN
EST
MORT

Dedié au Caffé Procope

pain, I am pleased that I have lived them, since they have brought me to see our present situation." He was referring to the new government that had been formed that spring with Washington as its President. Franklin tried to continue an autobiography he had started while in England, but between his pain and the drugs which he was given to ease it, he did not complete the book. It covers his life until his arrival in London in his fifty-first year, and then ends abruptly.

A few days before Franklin died, his doctor said, "he rose from his bed and begged that it be made up for him so that he might die in a decent manner. His daughter told him she hoped he would recover and live for many years longer. He calmly replied, 'I hope not.'"

Death came on April 17, 1790, eighty-four years and three months after he was born. Twenty thousand people escorted Benjamin Franklin to his grave beside Deborah in the Christ Church burying ground in Philadelphia. Many in the procession were famous by virtue of their positions in organizations and institutions Franklin had founded. The House of Representatives, which Franklin was instrumental in fashioning, declared a one-month period of mourning. On that day, when the senior—and perhaps the greatest—statesman of this country was buried, all Americans fell heir to a golden legacy of freedom that is worth more each succeeding year.

being the Declaration of Independence, the treaty with France, and the peace treaty with England. He had a hand in drafting them all and was the prime mover in the treaties.

The one-time printer's apprentice lived for another three years after the Constitutional Convention, but that gathering was his last appearance on the national scene. More and more restricted by his infirmities, he spent most of the last year of his life in bed. "For my own personal ease," he wrote to George Washington in September, 1789, "I should have died two years ago; but, though these years have been spent in excruciating

ACKNOWLEDGMENTS

The Editors are indebted to the following individuals and institutions for their generous advice and assistance in preparing this book:

The American Philosophical Society, Philadelphia—Richard H. Shryock, Mrs. Gertrude D. Hess
Atwater Kent Museum, Philadelphia—M. J. McCosker, Margaret P. Collins
Gertrudis Feliu, Claire de Forbin, Paris
The Free Library of Philadelphia—Ellen Shaffer
Historical Society of Pennsylvania—Nicholas B. Wainright
Insurance Company of North America, Philadelphia— C. A. Palmer
The Library Company of Philadelphia—Edwin Wolf, II
Philadelphia Museum of Art—Gertrude Toomey
Princeton University Library—Earle E. Coleman
Suzanne Puddefoot, London
Yale University Art Gallery—Caroline Rollins
Yale University Library—Leonard W. Labaree, Ralph L. Ketcham, Helen C. Boatfield, Helene H. Fineman

The photographs on pages 13 (bottom), 48, and 49 (left) were furnished through the courtesy of Yale University Library. The photograph of the Franklin hand press on page 31 is reproduced with the permission of the Rhode Island Historical Society and the Massachusetts Charitable Mechanic Association. The water color on page 77 was furnished through the courtesy of the Museum of the City of New York. The print of Bethlehem on page 91 is reproduced through the courtesy of Herbert Orth, *The Life History of the United States*, © Time, Inc.

ATWATER KENT MUSEUM

AMERICAN HERITAGE PUBLISHING CO., INC.

PRESIDENT JAMES PARTON
EDITORIAL DIRECTOR JOSEPH J. THORNDIKE, JR.
EDITOR, BOOK DIVISION RICHARD M. KETCHUM
ART DIRECTOR IRWIN GLUSKER

AMERICAN HERITAGE JUNIOR LIBRARY

MANAGING EDITOR RUSSELL BOURNE
ART DIRECTOR EMMA LANDAU
ASSOCIATE EDITOR WADE GREENE
ASSISTANT EDITOR DENNIS A. DINAN
CHIEF PICTURE RESEARCHER JULIA POTTS GREHAN
PICTURE RESEARCHER MARY LEVERTY
COPY EDITOR PATRICIA C. FROME
EDITORIAL ASSISTANT MARY GLOYNE PAYNE
EDITORIAL ASSISTANT NANCY SIMON

FOR FURTHER READING

The American Heritage Book of the Revolution. New York, American Heritage Publishing Co., 1958.

Andrews, Charles M., *The Colonial Background of the American Revolution.* New Haven, Yale University Press, 1939.

Becker, Carl, *Benjamin Franklin.* Ithaca, Cornell University Press, 1946.

Bemis, Samuel Flagg, *The Diplomacy of the American Revolution.* New York, Appleton, 1935.

Brewster, William, *The Pennsylvania and New York Frontier.* New York, George S. MacManus Co., 1954.

Bruce, William C., *Benjamin Franklin, Self-Revealed.* 2 vols. New York, Putnam, 1917.

Cohen, I. Bernard, *Benjamin Franklin: His Contribution to the American Tradition.* New York, Bobbs-Merrill, 1953.

Crane, Verner W., *Benjamin Franklin and a Rising People.* Boston, Little, Brown and Co., 1954.

Donovan, Frank, *The Benjamin Franklin Papers.* New York, Dodd, Mead and Co., 1962.

Dunway, Wayland F., *A History of Pennsylvania.* New Jersey, Prentice, 1948.

Franklin, Benjamin, *Autobiography and Selections from His Other Writings.* New York, The Modern Library, 1950.

Labaree, Leonard W., editor, *The Papers of Benjamin Franklin.* 6 vols. New Haven, Yale University Press, 1959-60.

Parton, James, *Life and Times of Benjamin Franklin.* 2 vols. New York, Ticknor, 1867.

Rossiter, Clinton, *Seedtime of the Republic.* New York, Harcourt, Brace and Company, 1953.

Russell, Francis, *Lexington, Concord, and Bunker Hill.* New York, American Heritage Junior Library, 1963.

Van Doren, Carl, *Benjamin Franklin.* New York, Viking Press, 1956.

Van Doren, Carl, editor, *Benjamin Franklin's Autobiographical Writings.* New York, Viking Press, 1945.

Wahlke, John C., editor, *Causes of the American Revolution.* Boston, D. C. Heath and Company, 1950.

Wright, Louis B., *The Cultural Life of the America Colonies, 1607-1763.* New York, Harper & Brothers, 1957.

Index

Bold face indicates pages
on which illustrations appear